Map Key

P9-DGS-184

Pacific Crest Trail
SOUTHERN
CALIFORNIA

DAVID MONEY HARRIS

 **WILDERNESS PRESS** ... *on the trail since 1967*

Day & Section Hikes Pacific Crest Trail: Southern California

1st EDITION 2012

Copyright © 2012 by David Money Harris

Front cover photos copyright © 2012 by the author
Interior photos, except where noted, by the author
Maps: David Money Harris and Scott McGrew
Cover design: Scott McGrew
Book design and layout: Ian Szymkowiak/Palace Press International
Editor: Laura Shauger

ISBN 978-0-89997-684-6

Manufactured in the United States of America

Published by: **Wilderness Press**
              Keen Communications
              PO Box 43673
              Birmingham, AL 35243
              (800) 443-7227
              info@wildernesspress.com
              www.wildernesspress.com

Visit our website for a complete listing of our books and for ordering information.
Distributed by Publishers Group West

Cover photos: Main: Delamar Mountain with Big Bear Lake and San Gorgonio Mountain in the distance (Hike 15). *Inset:* Crossing Whitewater River below San Gorgonio (Hike 13). *Frontispiece:* Twilight on the Kern River (Hike 30)

SAFETY NOTICE: Although Wilderness Press and the author have made every attempt to ensure that the information in this book is accurate at press time, they are not responsible for any loss, damage, injury, or inconvenience that may occur to anyone while using this book. You are responsible for your own safety and health while in the wilderness. The fact that a trail is described in this book does not mean that it will be safe for you. Be aware that trail conditions can change from day to day. Always check local conditions, know your own limitations, and consult a map.

Dedication

To Jennifer, Benjamin, Samuel, and Abraham

Deep Creek (Hike 18)

Table of Contents

Part 4: San Gabriel Mountains 103

Part 5: Southern Sierra 143

Preface

WELCOME TO THE PACIFIC CREST TRAIL! One of America's National Scenic Trails, the PCT runs 2,650 miles from Mexico to Canada along the mountainous backbone of California, Oregon, and Washington. This trail boasts the greatest elevation change and the most diverse scenery of any of the National Scenic Trails.

Each year, roughly 500 thru-hikers venture forth with the intent of hiking the entire PCT, leaving behind jobs and loved ones for the five-month journey. Several excellent books, including the three-volume *Pacific Crest Trail* series from Wilderness Press, help these hardy folks find their way.

But every year, tens of thousands of other hikers set foot on the PCT to hike for an hour, a day, or a weekend. This guide is part of a four-volume series written for day and section hikers seeking a casual excursion or moderate backpacking trip on one of our nation's most famous trails.

Even when I am hiking for just a few hours on the PCT, the question "What if I kept going?" invariably springs to mind. The romance of thru-hiking is unquestionably part of the allure of the trail. But I have young children and responsibilities at work, and this is not yet the right time in my life to be out for an extended journey. Most of us have similar constraints and can only spare a day or two or perhaps a long weekend at a time to answer the call of the wild. Thankfully, the PCT has dozens of segments offering hiking as fine as anywhere else in Southern California. This book features many of the best trips along the PCT between the Mexican border and the High Sierra. I have personally walked every trip in this book carrying a GPS receiver to log the trail. I have also walked a few segments that were not so satisfying and which I did not cover in this book.

The Pacific Crest Trail was first envisioned in the 1930s by Clinton Clarke, who pictured it as "traversing the best scenic areas and maintaining an absolute wilderness character." Clark founded the Pacific Crest Trail Conference, with members including the Boy Scouts, YMCA, and Ansel Adams, to plan and advocate for the trail. More than 40 YMCA groups spent the summers of 1935 to 1938 planning and exploring the route from Mexico to Canada. Today's trail largely follows the path pioneered by these young trailblazers. In 1968, Congress passed the National Trail Systems Act that established the Appalachian Trail and PCT as the first National Scenic Trails, "extended trails so located as to provide for maximum outdoor recreation potential and for the conservation and enjoyment of nationally significant scenic, historic, natural, or cultural qualities." A bold 18-year-old adventurer was the first to hike the entire contiguous distance, and his travel yarn, *The High Adventures of Eric Ryback*, tells a romantic story of his 1970 journey. In 1976, Teddi Boston, a 49-year-old mother of four, became the first woman to hike the entire distance solo. However, despite these groundbreaking trips, tremendous work remained to secure a right-of-way and construct nearly a thousand miles of trail. The trail was declared officially complete in 1993, but work continues even today to improve and protect it.

The Pacific Crest Trail Conference evolved into the Pacific Crest Trail Association (PCTA) in 1992. Today, the PCTA is a nonprofit organization that stewards the trail under a memorandum of understanding with the U.S. Forest Service, National Park Service, and Bureau of Land Management. The PCTA protects, preserves, and promotes the trail. Some of their key activities include trail maintenance, protecting the trail from urban encroachment and the scars of resource extraction, and sharing trail information. The staff at the PCTA was tremendously helpful while I was researching this guide. The royalties from this book will be donated to the PCTA to care for the trail. If you enjoy hiking on the PCT, you may find volunteering on a trail crew deeply satisfying. For more information, see **www.pcta.org**.

Several individuals have contributed ideas or reviews that have improved this book. They include Tony Condon, Sally Harris, Anitra Kass, Joe Sheehy, Elizabeth Thomas, and Fritz Ward. Also, numerous students from the Claremont Colleges On the Loose outdoor club have joined me scouting the trails.

I am indebted to my editors, Roslyn Bullas, Molly Merkle, and Laura Shauger for envisioning this series, inviting me to write this book, and helping bring the guide to completion. Designer Scott McGrew transformed the GPS data I gathered into useful maps. Annie Long did a terrific job with the page layout.

This book could not have happened without the support of my wife Jennifer. She and our young sons joined me for several of the shorter trips, and she was patient and encouraging as I spent numerous weekends away doing fieldwork for the longer trips.

Agua Caliente Creek (Hike 6)

Recommended Hikes

Introduction

How to Use This Guidebook

THE OVERVIEW MAP on the inside front cover will help you find the general location of each hike. The summary of all of the hikes on the facing page will help you compare trips and choose one.

Each trip begins with a short summary, including scenery, difficulty, solitude, and suitability for children (on a five-point scale, with five indicating the most scenic, difficult, solitary, and child-friendly hikes); distance; elevation gain; hiking time; the best season to go; recommended maps; and the trip's outstanding features. Hiking time accounts only for the time spent actually walking; most hikers will want to add time for lunch and breaks.

TRAIL MAPS

Each trip description contains a map showing the trailhead, route, and notable features in the area. A map legend detailing the symbols on the maps appears on the inside back cover.

The Global Positioning System (GPS) coordinates for the trail-heads and key landmarks are shown on the maps. Although the PCT is generally marked well enough that a GPS receiver is overkill in normal situations, satellite navigation may help you drive to the trail-head or find your way back in a whiteout.

ELEVATION PROFILES

Each trip also contains a detailed elevation profile to help you visualize how the trail rises and falls.

COMMERCIAL TOPOGRAPHIC MAPS

For all but the easiest hikes, it is prudent to know more about the surroundings than a map on one page of this book can show. Hikers

South Sierra Wilderness boundary (Hike 31)

have a variety of options to purchase commercial topographic maps with different coverage, detail, and pricing.

The U.S. Forest Service (USFS) has produced a colorful PCT map set. *Volume 1* covers the Mexican border to Big Bear Lake (Parts 1 and 2 of this book). *Volume 2* covers Big Bear to Tehachapi (Parts 3 and 4). *Volume 3* covers the Sierra Nevada (Part 5). These maps can be found at outdoor equipment stores or at **www.pcta.org.**

For those expecting to make multiple visits to a region exploring trails beyond the PCT, Tom Harrison's series of topographic maps are more versatile and convenient. These sturdy, color waterproof maps accurately portray all of the trails in the regions. Most of the trips in this guide are covered by Tom Harrison Maps; where applicable, the name of the map is noted on the trip description. These maps are also available at outdoor equipment stores and at **http:// tomharrisonmaps.com**.

Hikers in the San Jacinto region are fortunate to have the *Santa Rosa and San Jacinto Mountains National Monument* map. This well-designed map covers both desert and mountains and will give you ideas for dozens of great hikes across the monument year-round. The map is sold at ranger stations and hiking stores in the vicinity of the monument.

Erik the Black's *Pacific Crest Trail Atlas* is a handy five-volume book containing maps, distances, and data regarding water and camping. Volume 1 covers the region between the Mexican border and Tehachapi Pass (Parts 1–4 of this book), while Volume 2 covers the Sierra Nevada.

Veteran hikers are accustomed to referring to U.S. Geological Survey maps. Unfortunately, the PCT is new enough in many areas that the USGS maps often do not show the trail. Moreover, the other maps recommended in this section are more cost-effective and convenient to use.

A hiker by the trail name of Halfmile has developed an excellent set of PCT maps that can be freely downloaded for personal use and printed at your own computer. Halfmile's maps are based on the USGS maps but have the PCT and other key landmarks annotated. GPS users can also download GPS waypoints and tracks from the Halfmile site. The maps and data are found at **www.pctmap.net.**

Another hiker by the trail name of Postholer has posted a handy Google Map of the trail at: **http://postholer.com/gmap/gmap.php.**

Permits

Hikers should be aware of several permit requirements. The national forests in Southern California have instituted a Forest Adventure Pass system that requires vehicles parked on most national forest land to display a permit. This regulation applies to the majority of hikes in this book. The Forest Service aggressively tickets vehicles failing to display the pass at popular trailheads. A pass costs $5 for the day or $30 for the year. You may be able to purchase an adventure pass at a ranger station or business near the trailhead, although this approach can be problematic if you plan to start early. Alternatively, you can order a permit from the Forest Service by mail or on the Internet. Outdoor enthusiasts may find the Interagency Annual Pass to be a better value. This $80 pass covers entry fees to national parks and other federal lands, as well as substituting for a Forest Adventure Pass.

A California Campfire Permit is required to use a stove or campfire outside of developed campgrounds throughout the state. The free permit is valid for one year and can be obtained online or in person from Forest Service and BLM offices, **www.fs.fed.us/r5/ sequoia/passespermits/campfire_permit/campfire-index.html.**

The San Jacinto Wilderness has additional wilderness permit regulations for day and overnight use. See the trips in Part 2 for more details. The popular Humber Park Trailhead has a quota that fills up about a month in advance, so plan ahead.

Dogs on leash are allowed on all trails in this book except in the San Jacinto State Park wilderness (Hikes 9, 11, and 12). Leave aggressive dogs at home to avoid harassing the wildlife and other hikers.

Hazards

WE ARE MORTAL BEINGS. Like any other activity or lack of activity, hiking carries risks of injury or death. Fortunately, you can largely control the risks with prudent planning and behavior.

Always notify a relative or friend about your itinerary so that he or she can call for help if you are overdue. Hiking in a group is safer than hiking alone. If somebody is injured, part of the group can go for help while other group members stay with the injured person.

Carry plenty of water; plan on roughly one quart per five miles on a cool day and more in the heat. Dehydration can lead to heatstroke and kidney failure. An unfortunate PCT thru-hiker in April 2011 collapsed from dehydration at the end of the first day on the trail, earning himself the unfortunate trail name of Speed Bump.

If you need to resupply with water from a stream or other source, treat it before drinking. Many of the streams in the United States are now contaminated with giardia, cryptosporidium, and other nasty bugs that cause days of uncontrollable vomiting and diarrhea. Use a water filter, boil the water, or treat the water with iodine or a SteriPEN before drinking.

Bring sun protection. The sun is strong in California, and you burn faster in the mountains because there is less atmosphere to protect you. Wear a hat and sunglasses and apply sunscreen generously.

Carry a map and compass or GPS receiver. Be aware of your surroundings, and be sure you know how to retrace your steps to the start. It is hard to get too badly lost as long as you stay on the PCT. If you are lost, stay put and wait for help rather than wandering aimlessly. A campfire can help signal rescuers, but beware: A careless fire can get out of control and become a catastrophic wildfire. It doesn't hurt to carry a cell phone, but don't count on coverage in the mountains.

Pay attention to the weather forecast before you go, and bring appropriate gear. Southern California weather can be unpredictable, especially in the mountains, so bring a bit extra to handle a surprise.

Carry emergency gear sufficient to handle an unplanned night out on the trail. If a member of your group breaks a leg and it starts to rain, would you survive the night? Recommended gear includes warm waterproof clothing, a headlamp, a trash bag (for lightweight shelter), a whistle (to attract attention), and matches or a lighter. Cotton clothing loses its warmth when wet; synthetic fiber is a better choice.

Exercise caution when crossing streams, especially in high water during peak spring snowmelt or a thunderstorm. Hikers have been swept away and pinned down by raging creeks. If in doubt, turn back or seek shelter and wait for water levels to drop.

In the springtime, the high mountains are covered in beautiful snow. Only hike in the snow and ice if you are carrying an ice axe and traction devices and know how to use them. Highly experienced hikers have slipped and fallen to their death while crampons are in their packs.

Southern California's chaparral has evolved to burn as part of its life cycle. Many of the trips in this book pass areas that have burned in the past decade, about half ignited by lightning and half by the carelessness or malice of humankind. Exercise extreme caution with campfires, stoves, and other open flames, especially in late summer and fall when the dry vegetation becomes a tinderbox. If you see signs of wildfire while hiking, promptly evacuate the area.

Close encounters with desert vegetation, especially cactus and yuccas, can be painful. Pay attention to your surroundings. A pair of tweezers can help remove cactus needles.

Learn to recognize and avoid poison oak, whose urushiol oil causes an intensely itchy rash. Poison oak has three leaves that are usually shiny green, but sometimes turn red. Remember the words of wisdom: "Leaves of three, let it be." If you accidentally make contact with it, vigorously wash your skin with water to remove the oil right away. If a rash develops (typically a few days after contact), calamine lotion or Benadryl may relieve the symptoms. In severe cases, contact your physician.

There are relatively few dangerous animals in Southern California. Mountain lions are shy and usually avoid humans; count yourself lucky if you see one in a lifetime of hiking. They have been known to attack humans on very rare occasions. Children and petite women are at greatest risk. Traveling in groups deters lion attacks (and many other dangers). If you are attacked, yell, stand your ground, and fight back.

Rattlesnakes will usually warn you before you get too close. Heed their warnings and leave them alone. Never put your hands

or feet where you haven't looked first; in particular, avoid stepping over a log onto a sleeping snake. Most rattlesnake bites involve inebriated young men playing with the snake. If you are bitten, seek immediate medical attention.

Bee and scorpion stings are rare and normally just

Treat rattlesnakes with a healthy respect and give them a wide berth.

irritating, but they can have nasty consequences if you are allergic. Allergic hikers should consult their doctor and carry (and know how to use) an Epi-Pen or other treatment kit.

Ticks inhabit brushy areas, especially in springtime. In addition to being disgusting bloodsuckers, they can carry Lyme disease, which causes fever, headache, and fatigue. Lyme disease can lead to severe complications if left untreated. Thoroughly inspect your body for ticks at the end of the day, especially if you've been hiking through high grass or brush. If you are bitten by a tick, promptly

Lucky hikers may encounter a tarantula on the trail. Tarantulas are harmless to humans. Please leave them alone so that they can go about their business.

remove it with fine-tipped tweezers. If the tick is attached to your skin for less than 24 hours, your risk of Lyme disease is very small. If you detect symptoms of Lyme disease, such as a fever or rash, consult your doctor.

You may face as much risk from your fellow human as from the beasts of the forest. During hunting season (especially October and November), wear bright colors, stay on the trail, and keep alert. Most ATV and motorbike riders are responsible, but a few have been known to recklessly and illegally stray onto the PCT. All considered, hiking is a relative safe activity, and you should be as concerned about accidents on the drive to the trail as you are about injury on the trail.

Trail Etiquette

A few simple rules of trail etiquette protect the trail and make the outdoor experience more enjoyable for everyone. By government regulation, the PCT is restricted to hikers and equestrians. Bicycles, strollers, and motorized vehicles are not allowed. The PCT was not constructed to handle mountain bike use. Parts of the trail have suffered severe damage from mountain bikes, requiring costly reconstruction and even rerouting. Report illegal bicycle or ATV use to the local ranger.

- Stay on the trail. Don't cut switchbacks. Straying from the trail creates a confusing maze of side paths and causes erosion.
- Leave no trace. Take only pictures and leave only footprints. Don't litter. If you see garbage, you can be a hero by carrying it out.
- Bury human waste at least 200 feet away from any water source.
- Neither fellow hikers nor wildlife enjoy being barked at or threatened by dogs. If your dog isn't trained to behave well on the trail, leave it at home.
- Don't feed the animals. Keep the wildlife wild.

Student Conservation Association trail crew working on the PCT

Hiking with Children

One of my greatest pleasures has been hiking with my children. Infants love the rhythmic motion of hiking and the comfort of being snuggled against a parent's chest. Toddlers and preschoolers enjoy new sights and the chance to explore. Hiking and camping is a healthy and fun way for families to bond.

Fun along the PCT

If you are new to hiking with children, start short and work your way up gradually. Listen to cues from the children. But don't worry about the storm before the calm as little ones fuss before they fall asleep. Infants are the most portable and may happily ride with you for much of the day once they become accustomed to the trail. Ages two through five are a bit more challenging because the child will want to walk but will get tired quickly. Keep the trips fun.

There are many products on the market for carrying your children on the trail. My personal favorite for ages ten months through three years is the Ergo. In this particular carrier, young children can ride on the front of your torso, while older ones prefer your back.

The Ergo holds your child close to your body, which is comforting for the child and helps your balance.

Other tips:

- Few children enjoy having sunscreen applied, but do so thoroughly anyway. And put a hat on them, if they'll tolerate one.
- Keep your children nearby. Don't let them wander off.
- Hold hands when near cacti, steep drops, or fast-moving creeks.

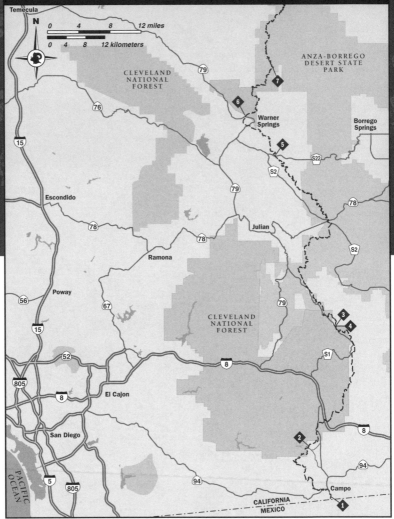

Temecula

N

0   4   8   12 miles
0 4 8   12 kilometers

CLEVELAND
NATIONAL
FOREST

ANZA-BORREGO
DESERT STATE
PARK

79

7

6

76

Warner
Springs

15

5

Borrego
Springs

S22

S2

Escondido

79

78

78

78

Julian

S2

Ramona

56

Poway

67

CLEVELAND
NATIONAL
FOREST

79

15

3

4

52

S1

805

8

8

El Cajon

San Diego

8

2

8

94

5

805

94

Campo

PACIFIC
OCEAN

1

CALIFORNIA
MEXICO

1

SAN DIEGO
BACKCOUNTRY

SCENERY: ☆ ☆ ☆	HIKING TIME: *10 hours or 2 days*
CHILDREN: ☆	BEST TIMES: *October–April*
DIFFICULTY: ☆ ☆ ☆ ☆	TOM HARRISON MAP: *San Diego Backcountry*
SOLITUDE: ☆ ☆ ☆ ☆	USFS PCT MAP: *Volume I*
DISTANCE: *20 miles (one-way with shuttle)*	OUTSTANDING FEATURES: *Start of the PCT*
ELEVATION GAIN: *2,900'*	

In April, hundreds of hikers from around the world make their way to a simple wooden monument at the Mexican border to begin their epic trek northward on the PCT to Canada. Although only about half reach their planned destination, none end their journey unchanged. This trip traces the first segment of the long journey. Though the trail weaves heavily around private ranchland, and the scenery is monotonous at times, the romance of the trip makes it hard to resist.

This trip is best hiked in the cool season, especially the winter or spring when Hauser Creek is likely to be running. Those hiking in April are likely to encounter a color-ful cast of thru-hikers beginning their PCT adventure. The Annual Day Zero PCT Kickoff (ADZPCTKO) party held at Lake Morena in late April is a particularly good time to do this trip; you can go see hikers talking about gear, water, and bears and give your well-wishes to this year's crew. See www.siechert.org/adz for more information, and make your reservations early if you want to join the fun.

If you plan to backpack this trip, be aware that in a typical year, there is no water available after March. Observant hikers will find small spots suitable for camping along the trail, with the best being alongside Hauser Creek. The section between Hauser Creek and Morena Butte is in Hauser Wilderness and technically requires a wilderness permit if you plan to camp overnight, but there is no good camping in this area anyway. Despite the mileage, the trip is gentle enough that day hiking makes an appealing alternative.

🚶🚶 From the PCT monument marking the southern terminus of the trail, look north down the hill for a signpost where the trail actually begins. Follow the trail for 1.1 miles to reach Forrest Gate

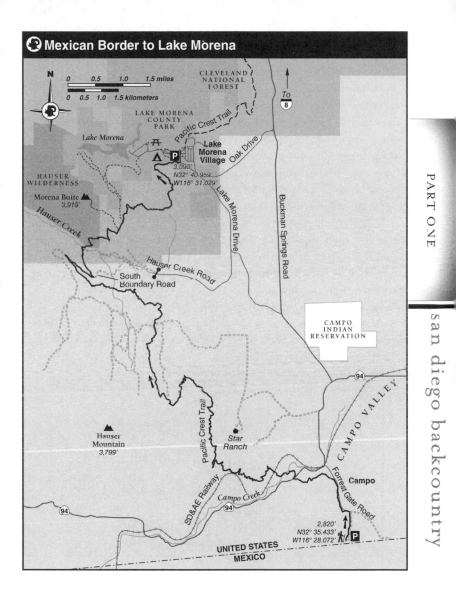

Mexican Border to Lake Morena

N

0   0.5   1.0   1.5 miles

0   0.5   1.0   1.5 kilometers

CLEVELAND NATIONAL FOREST

To 8

LAKE MORENA COUNTY PARK

Pacific Crest Trail

Lake Morena

Lake Morena Village

Oak Drive

3,090'
N32° 40.959'
W116° 31.029'

HAUSER WILDERNESS

Morena Butte
3,919'

Hauser Creek

Hauser Creek Road

South Boundary Road

Lake Morena Drive

Buckman Springs Road

CAMPO INDIAN RESERVATION

94

CAMPO VALLEY

Hauser Mountain
3,799'

Pacific Crest Trail

Star Ranch

SD&AE Railway

Campo Creek

94

94

Campo

Forrest Gate Road

2,820'
N32° 35.433'
W116° 28.072'

UNITED STATES
MEXICO

Rd. opposite a juvenile ranch facility. Hike north along the shoulder of the road for 0.2 mile to bypass private land in Campo until a sign indicates where the PCT veers off to the left (west).

Follow the trail through chaparral for 0.9 mile to cross Highway 94 and then cross seasonal Campo Creek on a wooden bridge. In another 0.7 mile, cross the tracks of the San Diego and Arizona Eastern Railroad. In 1.4 miles, cross another seasonal creek, watching out for the poison oak growing along the banks. The trail now follows a long and unremarkable course along the broad gentle shoulder of Hauser Mountain. As you pass through gates along the trail, be sure to close them behind you to keep cattle where they belong.

Pass above the historic oak-dotted Star Ranch. The slopes ahead burned in the Cowboy Fire of September 2010, an out-of-control signal fire started by disoriented illegal immigrants. The trail makes a long switchback to the south and crosses a jeep track, 4.3 miles from the creek, then another 2.0 miles beyond. Tolerable camping for small groups can be found in this area.

After rounding a corner, Morena Butte's granite walls come into view to the north. The trail makes a long detour westward above Hauser

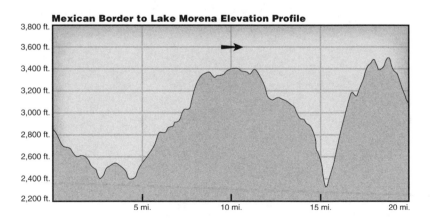

Mexican Border to Lake Morena Elevation Profile

Southern terminus of the PCT at the Mexican border fence

Canyon before dropping to South Boundary Rd. in 3.1 miles. Turn right and follow the dirt road 0.6 mile back to the east before a sign on the left points out the continuation of the PCT, which drops abruptly down rugged chaparral-clad slopes to reach Hauser Creek in 0.7 mile. Water is available here in the winter and spring, though it is often dry by April. Small but attractive campsites are located near the creek; beware of poison oak.

Cross the creek and a road on the far side marking the boundary of Hauser Wilderness. Switchback up steep sunbaked slopes. As you climb, enjoy the views westward to Barrett Lake, a reservoir for the city of San Diego. Reach a saddle southeast of Morena Butte in 1.5 miles. A small cairn marks the start of a milelong climber's trail to the summit, which offers great views (see Hike 2, page 19), but the PCT continues north. In 0.2 mile, stay right at a junction with an unmarked trail shortcutting to the lake. Climb to a weaving ridge and follow it 2.8 miles back to the trailhead outside Lake Morena County Park.

DIRECTIONS This trip requires an 8.5-mile car or bicycle shuttle. Arrange for a vehicle at Lake Morena County Park at the northern end of the trip. From Interstate 8, take Buckman Springs Rd. (Exit 51) south for 5.5 miles, and then turn right on Oak Dr. In 1.7 miles, turn right again onto Lake Morena Dr. Continue 0.8 mile to the park. Trailhead parking is on the left by the PCT sign at the entrance to the park. Those without annual adventure passes may prefer day-use parking in the park for $3.

To reach the southern trailhead, follow Lake Morena Dr. 4.0 miles southeast to Buckman Springs Rd. Turn right and go 1.5 miles to a T-junction with Highway 94. Turn right again and proceed 1.5 miles, then make a left on Forrest Gate Rd. This road eventually becomes dirt and passes under high-voltage lines. In 1.5 miles, turn left and then immediately right up a hill to reach the monument along the border fence at the southern terminus of the PCT. The U.S. Border Patrol recommends parking 0.1 mile northwest of the monument at a PCT sign.

PERMIT Forest Adventure Pass required outside Lake Morena County Park. Inside the park, you must pay a day-use fee.

This hike briefly passes through the extreme southeast corner of Hauser Wilderness. In the unlikely event that you wish to camp in the wilderness area, a free wilderness permit from the Cleveland National Forest is required.

OTHER POINTS OF INTEREST Lake Morena County Park offers convenient camping. Train buffs will enjoy the Pacific Southwest Railway Museum (www.sdrm.org) in Campo, which features historic train rides on select dates.

SCENERY: ✿ ✿ ✿
CHILDREN: ✿ ✿ ✿
DIFFICULTY: ✿ ✿ ✿
SOLITUDE: ✿ ✿ ✿
DISTANCE: *8 miles (out-and-back)*
ELEVATION GAIN: *1,500'*

HIKING TIME: *4 hours*
BEST TIMES: *October–May*
TOM HARRISON MAP: San Diego Backcountry
USFS PCT MAP: Volume I
OUTSTANDING FEATURES: *Views*

Morena Butte is an attractive granite outcrop overlooking Lake Morena. This moderate hike follows the PCT from the lake to the flank of the mountain, and then takes a straightforward climber's path to the summit. Go on a cool clear day to enjoy the panoramic views. The origin of the butte's name is lost in history. It may come from the Spanish word for "brown" or may honor an early settler of the region.

🥾🥾 From the PCT trailhead outside Lake Morena County Park, hike southwest on the PCT to gain the tip of a ridge. The trail meanders through chaparral up the hillside, offering views of the lake as you

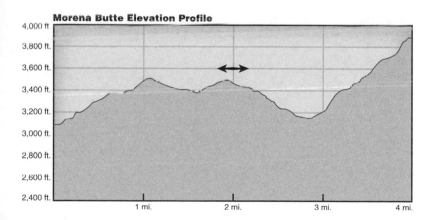

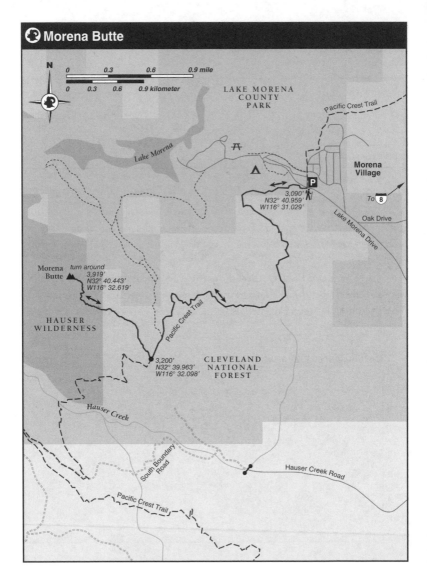

Morena Butte

N

0   0.3   0.6   0.9 mile
0   0.3   0.6   0.9 kilometer

LAKE MORENA
COUNTY
PARK

Pacific Crest Trail

Lake Morena

Morena
Village

To 8

3,090'
N32° 40.959'
W116° 31.029'

Oak Drive

Lake Morena Drive

Morena
Butte

turn around
3,919'
N32° 40.443'
W116° 32.619'

Pacific Crest Trail

HAUSER
WILDERNESS

3,200'
N32° 39.963'
W116° 32.098'

CLEVELAND
NATIONAL
FOREST

Hauser Creek

South Boundary Road

Hauser Creek Road

Pacific Crest Trail

climb. In 2.8 miles, pass an unmarked trail on the right leading back to the lake. In another 0.2 mile, reach a high point of the trail on the east flank of Morena Butte. Look for a small cairn marking a climber's trail that leads west 1.0 mile up the butte. The trail is mostly straightforward, but becomes harder to follow near the summit where it crosses slabs of granite. Watch for cairns (piles of rock) marking the route.

Morena Butte has three distinct summits. The trail leads to the first one, which is the highest. The other two summits are also easy to reach and offer their own unique vistas.

On the return, you may consider making a semiloop by taking the unmarked Morena Butte and Ward's Flat Trail that you passed on the way up. It leads north through a pleasant glen and then joins a road that takes you back along the shore of Lake Morena.

DIRECTIONS   From Interstate 8, take Buckman Springs Rd. (Exit 51) south for 5.5 miles, and then turn right on Oak Dr. In 1.7 miles, turn right again onto Lake Morena Dr. Continue 0.8 mile to Lake Morena County Park. Trailhead parking is on the left by the PCT sign at the entrance to the park. Those without annual adventure passes may prefer day-use parking in the park for $3.

PERMIT   Forest Adventure Pass or county park day-use fee required.

OTHER POINTS OF INTEREST   Lake Morena County Park offers convenient camping.

3 Indian Creek Loop

SCENERY: ⭐ ⭐ ⭐ ⭐	HIKING TIME: *4 hours*
CHILDREN: ⭐ ⭐	BEST TIMES: *All year*
DIFFICULTY: ⭐ ⭐ ⭐	TOM HARRISON MAP: San Diego Backcountry
SOLITUDE: ⭐ ⭐	USFS PCT MAP: Volume I
DISTANCE: *9 miles (loop)*	OUTSTANDING FEATURES: *Diverse scenery*
ELEVATION GAIN: *1,000'*	

Laced with a web of trails, Laguna Mountain National Recreation Area in Cleveland National Forest is a playground for San Diego–area outdoor lovers. Perched atop a mile-high ridge, the trails are usually enjoyable year-round, although they may be hot in midsummer or icy after a winter storm. This popular hike combines the Noble Canyon and Indian Creek Trails with the PCT to form an appealing loop through many different ecosystems. The area was devastated by fire in 2002 and 2003, but this hike remains enjoyable.

🚶🚶 This trip starts on the west side of Sunrise Highway at the Penny Pines Trailhead. The trailhead is named for the Penny Pines program, started in California in 1941, in which private donations are raised for planting new trees in burned-over areas. Be sure you are on the right trail; several others start in the same area. Follow the signed Noble Canyon Trail west. The Noble Canyon Trail is popular with mountain bikers, who consider the lower segment to be one of the technical classics of Southern California. However, the gentle upper segment meanders through a forest of oak and pine.

Stay right at a fork in 0.1 mile. The trail soon reaches the edge of a vast burn area. In hot, dry, and windy October 2003, much of Southern California was aflame; it was the worst firestorm in recorded state history. The Cedar Fire was started by a lost hunter who lit a fire to signal rescuers. The blaze was driven by fierce Santa Ana winds and firefighters were stretched thin by *fourteen other major fires burning at the same time.* The Cedar Fire soon grew to consume

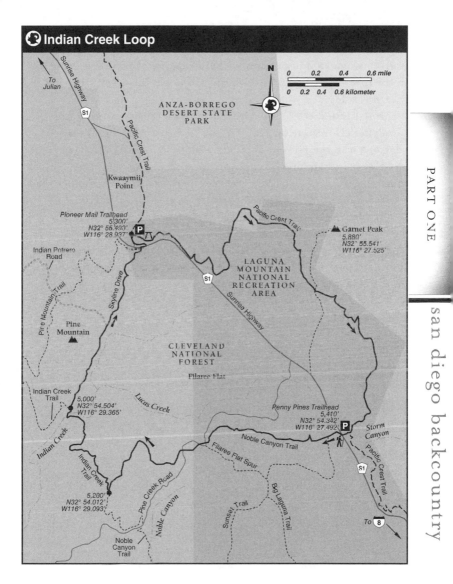

Indian Creek Loop

ANZA-BORREGO
DESERT STATE
PARK

To
Julian

S1

Sunrise Highway

Pacific Crest Trail

Kwaaymii
Point

Pioneer Mail Trailhead
5,300'
N32° 55.493'
W116° 28.937'

P

Indian Potrero
Road

Pine Mountain Trail

Skyline Drive

Pine
Mountain

Indian Creek
Trail

Indian Creek Trail

5,000'
N32° 54.504'
W116° 29.365'

Lucas Creek

Indian Creek Trail

5,200'
N32° 54.012'
W116° 29.093'

Noble Canyon Trail

Noble
Canyon
Trail

Noble Canyon

Pine Creek Road

Filaree Flat Spur

Sunset Trail

Filaree Flat

CLEVELAND
NATIONAL
FOREST

Pacific Crest Trail

Garnet Peak
5,880'
N32° 55.541'
W116° 27.525'

LAGUNA
MOUNTAIN
NATIONAL
RECREATION
AREA

Sunrise Highway

S1

Penny Pines Trailhead
5,410'
N32° 54.342'
W116° 27.492'

P

Storm
Canyon

Noble Canyon Trail

Big Laguna Trail

Pacific Crest Trail

S1

To 8

N

0   0.2   0.4   0.6 mile

0   0.2   0.4   0.6 kilometer

280,278 acres, killing 15 people and destroying 2,232 homes. The Laguna Mountains were one of the casualties of the fire. The trail leads through ribbonwood and other chaparral that is recovering well in the first stage of plant succession. However, the forests may not return for decades.

In 1.1 miles, cross Pine Creek Rd., then recross it twice more soon after. Continue on Noble Canyon as it climbs slightly onto the edge of a hill, then descends to meet Indian Creek Trail. Turn right and follow Indian Creek Trail northwest through a burn area for 1.0 mile to reach the grass-lined creek. Indian Creek is rarely more than a trickle. Drinking the untreated water is *not* recommended.

Immediately after crossing the creek, leave the trail and turn right onto defunct jeep tracks. Follow the tracks up a steep hill, then alongside a grassy meadow. The tracks improve into a dirt road (not shown on park maps). Pass various side roads as you head northeast on the main road. In 1.3 miles, reach Sunset Highway at a junction with Pine Mountain Trail.

Cross the highway, jog right, and follow a paved road down to Pioneer Mail Trailhead, where you'll find an outhouse, picnic tables,

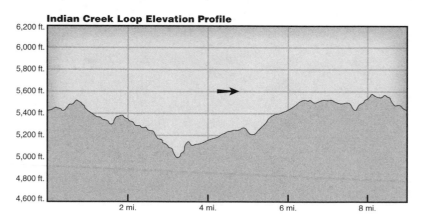

Indian Creek Loop Elevation Profile

Majestic oak and pine trees survived the Cedar Fire.

and access to the Pacific Crest Trail. At the trailhead sign, pick up
the southbound PCT, which leads below the picnic area before
climbing around a hill overlooking Cottonwood Canyon. This side
of the highway burned in the Pines Fire in August 2002. The dramatic views down the steep eastern escarpment of the Laguna Mountains into the Anza-Borrego Desert continue to improve as you walk.
In 2.6 miles, reach a junction with Garnet Peak Trail.

The optional excursion to Garnet Peak is highly recommended.
It adds 1.2 miles and 500 feet of elevation gain round-trip. If you
choose to make it, turn left and follow Garnet Peak Trail up to the
summit; see Hike 4 (page 27) for more details. After enjoying the
views, return to the PCT.

Continue south on the PCT. The trail approaches the edge of the scarp from time to time, offering impressive vistas back toward Garnet Peak's steep face and over Storm Canyon into the desert below. The Kumeyaay band of Native Americans made the trek each spring up this rugged canyon to their summer hunting grounds in the Laguna Mountains. In 1.4 miles, reach a trail junction. The PCT veers left, but this trip turns right onto Big Laguna and Noble Canyon Trail, which in 0.1 mile arrives back at Penny Pines Trailhead.

DIRECTIONS From Interstate 8 east of San Diego, take Exit 47 north on Sunrise Highway (County Road S-1). Proceed 14 miles to Penny Pines Trailhead on the shoulder of the highway at mile marker 27.3.

PERMIT Forest Adventure Pass required.

OTHER POINTS OF INTEREST The heavily visited Laguna Mountain National Recreation Area is laced with a variety of other trails. Check in at the Mt. Laguna Visitor Information Center on Sunrise Highway for maps and suggestions. Popular campsites in the area include Laguna and Burnt Rancheria. Remote camping is allowed along the back roads outside the recreation area; a free permit from the Cleveland National Forest is required.

4 Garnet Peak

SCENERY: ✿ ✿ ✿	HIKING TIME: *2 hours*
CHILDREN: ✿ ✿ ✿ ✿	BEST TIMES: *All year*
DIFFICULTY: ✿ ✿	TOM HARRISON MAP: San Diego Backcountry
SOLITUDE: ✿ ✿	USFS PCT MAP: Volume I
DISTANCE: *4 miles (out–and–back or loop)*	OUTSTANDING FEATURES: *Vistas from the peak*
ELEVATION GAIN: *600'*	

Garnet Peak is an easy introduction to the pleasures of Laguna Mountain National Recreation Area. The peak is named for the gems that were once mined in this area. Its 5,900-foot summit offers outstanding views over Anza–Borrego Desert.

This trip follows the Pacific Crest Trail to Garnet Peak Trail to Garnet Peak. You may return the way you came, or may shorten the trip and get a change of scenery by descending Garnet Peak Trail straight to Sunrise Highway. If you choose the latter option, you may wish to leave a bicycle or second vehicle at Garnet Peak Trailhead or may walk back a half mile along the shoulder of the highway.

🚶🚶 A confusing web of trails radiates from Penny Pines Trail-head. Walk east on the Big Laguna Trail for 0.1 mile to meet the

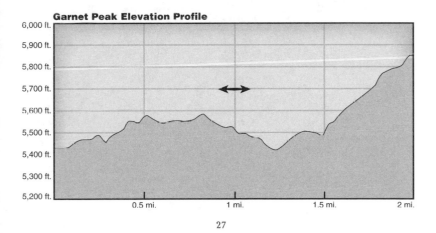

Garnet Peak Elevation Profile

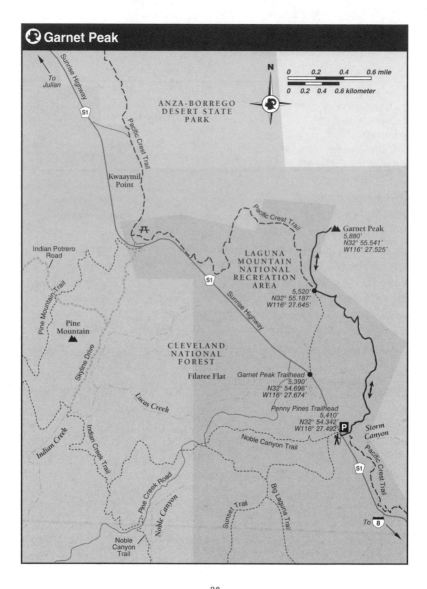

Garnet Peak

To Julian

Sunrise Highway

S1

Pacific Crest Trail

Kwaaymil Point

ANZA-BORREGO
DESERT STATE
PARK

N

| 0 | 0.2 | 0.4 | 0.6 mile |

| 0 | 0.2 | 0.4 | 0.6 kilometer |

Pacific Crest Trail

Garnet Peak
5,880'
N32° 55.541'
W116° 27.525'

LAGUNA
MOUNTAIN
NATIONAL
RECREATION
AREA

Indian Potrero
Road

Pine Mountain Trail

S1

Sunrise Highway

5,520'
N32° 55.187'
W116° 27.645'

Pine
Mountain

Skyline Drive

CLEVELAND
NATIONAL
FOREST

Filaree Flat

Garnet Peak Trailhead
5,390'
N32° 54.696'
W116° 27.674'

Lucas Creek

Penny Pines Trailhead
5,410'
N32° 54.342'
W116° 27.492'

P

Storm
Canyon

Indian Creek

Indian Creek Trail

Noble Canyon Trail

Pacific Crest Trail

S1

Pine Creek Road

Noble Canyon

Sunset Trail

Big Laguna Trail

To 8

Noble
Canyon
Trail

Ice-encrusted chaparral on Garnet Peak

PCT. Turn left (north) and follow the PCT along the rim of Storm Canyon. Soon you will see the steep lichen-covered face of Garnet Peak to the north. In 1.4 miles, reach a four-way junction. Turn right and climb 0.6 mile to the summit of Garnet Peak.

Looking east over Anza-Borrego Desert, you may pick out the historic Butterfield Stage Route by which U.S. Post Office mail was carried from Los Angeles to St. Louis from 1858 to 1861, when the Civil War severed the route. Wells Fargo continued stagecoach service to serve mining camps until the completion of the Transcontinental Railroad in 1869.

After enjoying the view, return to the four-way junction. Either continue straight for 0.6 mile to reach Garnet Peak Trailhead, or turn left and follow the PCT back to Penny Pines Trailhead.

Garnet Peak

DIRECTIONS   From Interstate 8 east of San Diego, take Exit 47 north on Sunrise Highway (County Road S-1). Proceed 14 miles to Penny Pines Trailhead on the shoulder of the highway at mile marker 27.3. If you would like to make a loop, you will descend to Garnet Peak Trailhead, which can be found 0.5 mile farther north along the highway at mile marker 27.8.

PERMIT   Forest Adventure Pass required.

OTHER POINTS OF INTEREST   The heavily visited Laguna Mountain National Recreation Area is laced with a variety of other trails. Check at the Mt. Laguna Visitor Information Center on Sunrise Highway for maps and suggestions. Popular campsites in the area include Laguna and Burnt Rancheria. Remote camping is allowed along the back roads outside the recreation area; a free permit from the Cleveland National Forest is required.

5 Eagle Rock

SCENERY: ☆ ☆ ☆ ☆ ☆	HIKING TIME: *4 hours*
CHILDREN: ☆ ☆ ☆	BEST TIMES: *All year*
DIFFICULTY: ☆ ☆ ☆	TOM HARRISON MAP: San Diego Backcountry
SOLITUDE: ☆ ☆ ☆	USFS PCT MAP: Volume I
DISTANCE: *8 miles (one-way)*	OUTSTANDING FEATURES: *Eagle Rock and spring*
ELEVATION GAIN: *700'*	*wildflowers*

*Eagle Rock, perched on a hill overlooking Warner Springs Ranch, bears a stunning
likeness to its namesake raptor. In April, the surrounding meadows explode with the
color of wildflowers. A walk along the oak-lined banks of Cañada Verde caps off this
magnificent hike.*

*This trip is described as a one-way hike from south to north with an 8-mile car or
bicycle shuttle. If only one vehicle is available, you can take the trip as a 6-mile out-and-
back hike from the fire station in Warner Springs. Although the hike can be done all year,
it is hot in summer and cold in winter.*

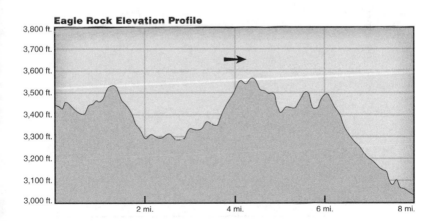

Eagle Rock Elevation Profile

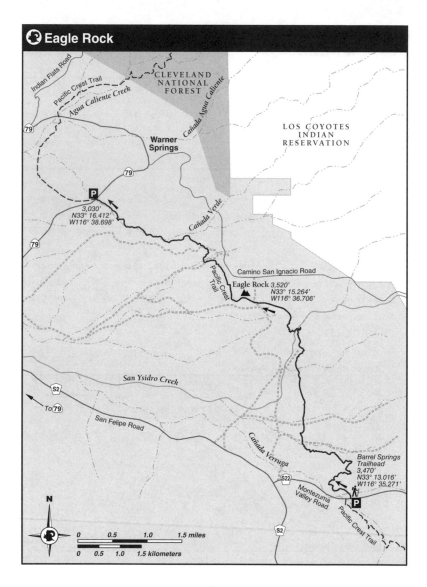

Eagle Rock

Indian Flats Road

Pacific Crest Trail

Agua Caliente Creek

Cañada Agua Caliente

CLEVELAND NATIONAL FOREST

79

Warner Springs

79

LOS COYOTES INDIAN RESERVATION

P

3,030'
N33° 16.412'
W116° 38.698'

Cañada Verde

79

Pacific Crest Trail

Camino San Ignacio Road

Eagle Rock 3,520'
N33° 15.264'
W116° 36.706'

San Ysidro Creek

S2

To 79

San Felipe Road

Cañada Verruga

S22

Montezuma Valley Road

Barrel Springs Trailhead
3,470'
N33° 13.016'
W116° 35.271'

P

Pacific Crest Trail

S2

N

0   0.5   1.0   1.5 miles

0   0.5   1.0   1.5 kilometers

Eagle Rock

🚶 From Barrel Springs Trailhead, cross to the north side of Highway S22 (Montezuma Valley Rd.) and pass through a gate with a PCT marker. Hikers must disregard the Vista Irrigation District's menacing NO TRESPASSING signs. This hike crosses active rangeland; be sure to close all gates behind you. The PCT crosses many jeep tracks and horse trails through the ranch but is regularly marked with signposts.

Briefly follow a powerline service road, and then veer right before curving back left to circle a ridge. The PCT weaves through a series of ridges as it crosses the rangeland. The hills are covered in chaparral, while the grassy valleys are dotted with the occasional oaks. Abundant spring wildflowers include blue lupine, pinkish-purple owl's clover, brilliant orange California poppies, and the aptly named California goldfields.

In 3.6 miles, the trail intersects San Ysidro Creek and follows it into a scenic canyon. It crosses the creek and climbs up the ridge on the far side. In another 1.4 miles, reach a cluster of granite rocks. A signed trail curves around to the backside, where Eagle Rock is clearly recognizable.

After enjoying Eagle Rock, continue along the PCT. March across another 1.8 miles of rangeland to reach Cañada Verde ("Green Ravine"). Follow the creek down an oak-lined canyon. In 1.2 miles, pass through a gate. In another 0.1 mile, the California Riding and Hiking Trail veers off to the right to reach the Warner Springs post office and ranch. However, this hike continues straight through a second gate. It soon crosses the creek and passes through a third gate to reach the highway by the fire station.

DIRECTIONS   Position one vehicle on Highway 79 in a turnout across from the California Department of Forestry fire station at the south end of Warner Springs (0.3 mile south of mile marker 79 SD 34.50.) To reach the second trailhead, continue south on Highway 79 for 2.5 miles. Turn left on San Felipe Rd. (Highway S2). In 4.8 miles, turn left onto Montezuma Valley Rd. (Highway S22). In 1.0 mile, park at Barrel Springs Trailhead in a large dirt lot on the right side near a PCT sign.

PERMIT   None

OTHER POINTS OF INTEREST   This trip can be combined with Agua Caliente Creek (Hike 6) for a two-day getaway. Overnight visitors may enjoy staying at historic Warner Springs Ranch (temporarily closed) or camping at Indian Flats Campground. Warner Springs Ranch has short trails for hiking, horseback riding, and mountain biking, as well as access to its famous hot springs resort. Indian Flats Campground, located 7 miles up winding Indian Flats Road, is first-come, first-served and is only open May 31 through Feb. 29 to protect habitat for the endangered arroyo toad.

6 Agua Caliente Creek

SCENERY: ✿ ✿ ✿	HIKING TIME: *4 hours*
CHILDREN: ✿ ✿ ✿	BEST TIMES: *October–May*
DIFFICULTY: ✿ ✿ ✿	TOM HARRISON MAP: San Diego Backcountry
SOLITUDE: ✿ ✿ ✿	USFS PCT MAP: Volume I
DISTANCE: *9 miles (out–and–back)*	OUTSTANDING FEATURES: *Creek*
ELEVATION GAIN: *1,100'*	

North of Warner Springs, the Pacific Crest Trail follows Agua Caliente Creek up a lovely canyon lined with sycamores, cottonwoods, and oaks. Visitors will enjoy frolicking in the creek or spending the night at the secluded, undeveloped campsites in the canyon. Although agua caliente *means "hot water," the nearest hot springs are at Warner Springs Ranch Resort.*

🐾 From the PCT parking area, cross to the north side of the highway and walk up an unmarked dirt road for 0.1 mile. Pass through a gate (this is active ranchland; be sure to close all gates behind you) and follow signs for the PCT.

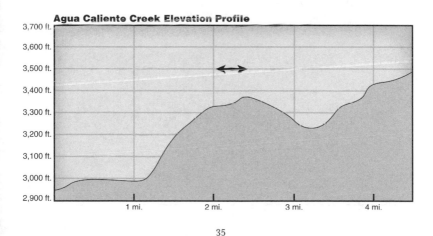

Agua Caliente Creek Elevation Profile

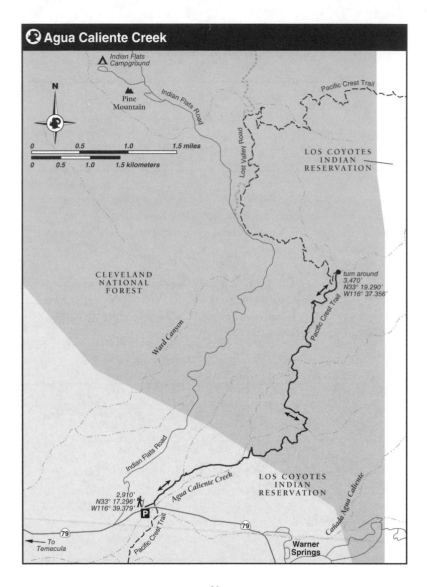

🌀 Agua Caliente Creek

Indian Flats
Campground

Pine
Mountain

Indian Flats Road

Pacific Crest Trail

Lost Valley Road

LOS COYOTES
INDIAN
RESERVATION

0   0.5   1.0   1.5 miles

0   0.5   1.0   1.5 kilometers

CLEVELAND
NATIONAL
FOREST

turn around
3,470'
N33° 19.290'
W116° 37.356'

Pacific Crest Trail

Ward Canyon

Indian Flats Road

2,910'
N33° 17.296'
W116° 39.379'

Agua Caliente Creek

LOS COYOTES
INDIAN
RESERVATION

Cañada Agua Caliente

P

79

Pacific Crest Trail

79

To
Temecula

Warner
Springs

Sugar bush in bloom

The PCT follows the west side of Agua Caliente Creek through a broad valley. Note that the California Riding and Hiking Trail parallels the PCT in this area but is wider, sandier, and better suited to equestrians. Several ranch roads also pass through the area, and the PCT is not always well marked. When in doubt, pick any path leading upstream, and you'll eventually rejoin the PCT. In 1.2 miles, reach a campground with a small bench. Warner Springs Ranch graciously allows PCT hikers to stay here, but small groups will find more appealing campsites farther upstream.

Cross the creek and cross the boundary into Cleveland National Forest. The trail climbs up into the chaparral-clad hills to bypass a narrow section of the canyon. You may see some unmarked side trails; stay on the PCT. In 1.9 miles, descend to rejoin the creek.

The next section of the hike is the most scenic. The trail generally stays close to the water, repeatedly crossing the creek. Several small clearings offer attractive campsites for groups with one to three tents. Note that campfires are not allowed, although campstoves are permitted except during periods of extreme fire danger. In 1.5 miles, the PCT leaves the creek and begins switchbacking up toward Indian Flats Road. This is a good place to turn around; the trail becomes steeper and less attractive beyond.

DIRECTIONS From Highway 79 on the northern outskirts of Warner Springs 0.2 mile south of mile marker 79 SD 37.00, park in a large turnout on the south side of the road.

PERMIT None

OTHER POINTS OF INTEREST This trip can be combined with Eagle Rock (Hike 5) for a two-day getaway. Overnight visitors may enjoy staying at historic Warner Springs Ranch (temporarily closed) or camping at Indian Flats Campground. Warner Springs Ranch has short trails for hiking, horseback riding, and mountain biking, as well as access to its famous hot springs resort. Indian Flats Campground, located 7 miles up winding Indian Flats Road, is first-come, first-served and is only open May 31 through Feb. 29 to protect habitat for the endangered arroyo toad.

7 Combs Peak

SCENERY: ✿ ✿ ✿
CHILDREN: ✿ ✿ ✿
DIFFICULTY: ✿ ✿
SOLITUDE: ✿ ✿ ✿ ✿
DISTANCE: *5 miles (out-and-back)*
ELEVATION GAIN: *1,200'*

HIKING TIME: *3 hours, possible overnight camp*
BEST TIMES: *October–May*
TOM HARRISON MAP: San Diego Backcountry
USFS PCT MAP: Volume I
OUTSTANDING FEATURES: *Remoteness and views*

Combs Peak is the high point of the Bucksnort Mountains, a remote minor range overlooking Anza–Borrego Desert State Park. The mountain was named for Jim Combs, a miner who worked the area in the 1890s. The ascent involves a 2-mile walk along the PCT to a saddle with camping opportunities, followed by a short but steep scramble up a climber's trail to the summit. Combs Peak draws a surprising number of hikers, who are rewarded with some of San Diego County's finest panoramic views. This trip is appealing throughout the cooler season, but the 6,193-foot peak may be icy right after a winter storm.

🚶🚶 Follow the PCT north from the trailhead. This area burned in the 2003 Coyote Fire, an 18,000-acre fire triggered by dry

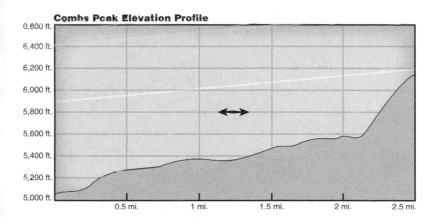

Combs Peak Elevation Profile

🌀 Combs Peak

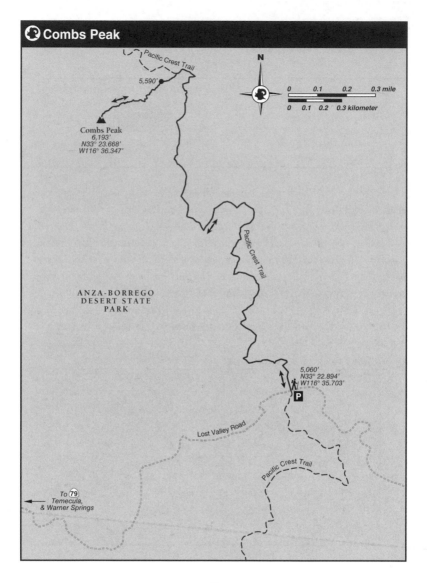

Pacific Crest Trail

5,590'

N

0   0.1   0.2   0.3 mile

0   0.1   0.2   0.3 kilometer

Combs Peak
6,193'
N33° 23.668'
W116° 36.347'

Pacific Crest Trail

ANZA-BORREGO
DESERT STATE
PARK

5,060'
N33° 22.894'
W116° 35.703'
P

Lost Valley Road

Pacific Crest Trail

To (79)
Temecula,
& Warner Springs

Looking toward Combs Peak from the Pacific Crest Trail

lightning. The chaparral has grown back rapidly, but the forest will take decades to return. The first portion leads through a beautiful stand of ribbonwood, readily identified by its flaky red bark, as well as scrub oak and manzanita. The trail makes a leisurely climb along the east flank of the mountains. In 1.0 mile, pass a charred stand of Coulter pines. In another mile, arrive at a saddle on the east spur of Combs Peak. Flat campsites can be found on the ridge just left of the trail, *but you must haul in all of your water.*

To reach the peak, look for a pile of rocks (called a duck or cairn) on the left side of the trail near the saddle marking the start of

Thomas Mountain, San Jacinto and the Desert Divide, and San Gorgonio from Combs Peak

the climber's trail. Follow a series of ducks west through the chaparral up the ridge. The trail is mostly clear but becomes obscure in places. If you seem off-route, look carefully for the next duck because staying on the climber's trail is far better than thrashing through the brush. After surmounting a steep step, reach the rocky summit. From here, you can look north over Anza Valley to the Desert Divide and San

Jacinto. Towering San Gorgonio stands farther north. Close by to the northeast is Toro Peak, the 8,716-foot high point of the Santa Rosa Mountains.

After enjoying the view from the top, retrace your steps to the trailhead.

DIRECTIONS   From Highway 79 between Temecula and Warner Springs near mile marker 79 SD 46.00, turn east onto Chihuahua Valley Rd. Proceed 6.4 miles to where the road makes a sharp right turn. Instead of turning, continue straight onto the dirt Lost Valley Rd. (not the private road on its left). In 5.1 miles, park at a saddle where the PCT crosses the road.

PERMIT   None

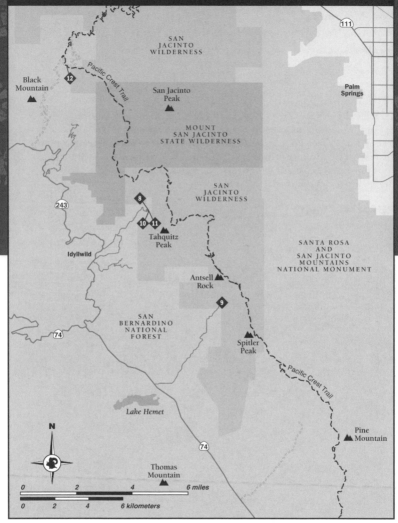

San Jacinto Mountains

SAN
JACINTO
WILDERNESS

Black
Mountain

San Jacinto
Peak

MOUNT
SAN JACINTO
STATE WILDERNESS

Palm
Springs

SAN
JACINTO
WILDERNESS

Pacific Crest Trail

243

Tahquitz
Peak

Idyllwild

SANTA ROSA
AND
SAN JACINTO
MOUNTAINS
NATIONAL MONUMENT

Antsell
Rock

SAN
BERNARDINO
NATIONAL
FOREST

Spitler
Peak

74

Pacific Crest Trail

Lake Hemet

N

Pine
Mountain

74

Thomas
Mountain

| 0 | | 2 | | 4 | | 6 miles |
| 0 | 2 | | 4 | | 6 kilometers | |

2

SAN JACINTO MOUNTAINS

8 Desert Divide

SCENERY: ✿ ✿ ✿ ✿ ✿	RECOMMENDED MAP: *Santa Rosa and*
CHILDREN: ✿	*San Jacinto Mountains National Monument*
DIFFICULTY: ✿ ✿ ✿ ✿ ✿	TOM HARRISON MAP: *San Jacinto Wilderness*
SOLITUDE: ✿ ✿ ✿	(only covers northern part)
DISTANCE: *21 miles (one-way with shuttle)*	USFS PCT MAP: Volume I
ELEVATION GAIN: *5,700'*	OUTSTANDING FEATURES: *Views and rugged*
HIKING TIME: *12 hours or 2—3 days*	*mountains*
BEST TIMES: *April—June, October—November*	

The Desert Divide is a long ridge running south from San Jacinto that separates the Los Angeles Basin from the desert. The divide is studded with a series of attractive granite peaks. This spectacular hike follows the PCT along the crest of the ridge. Peak baggers will enjoy exploring some of the summits found close to the trail. This trip may be done as a long day hike or as a 2—3 day backpacking trip. Availability of water is a consideration for backpackers, especially in the fall.

This was one of the most difficult sections of the PCT to construct. The legendary Sam Fink, a Santa Ana fire captain and long-time Sierra Club leader, spent a good part of the 1960s and 1970s chopping a route through the wiry chaparral along the crest of the divide. Turning his climber's route into the PCT took three more years of drilling, blasting, and cutting. Hikers now enjoy a well-engineered and straightforward trail along the formerly inaccessible divide.

🚶🚶 Hike up Devil's Slide Trail from Humber Park for 2.5 miles to meet the PCT at Saddle Junction. Turn sharply right and follow the PCT south through a splendid forest. In 1.4 miles, reach a junction with South Ridge Trail to Tahquitz Peak. It is worth making this easy excursion to the summit to study the route ahead. To reach the peak, turn right on South Ridge Trail and proceed 0.4 mile, then follow a short spur to the lookout on the summit. Your efforts are rewarded with a stunning view of the granite-toothed Desert Divide leading south. Then return to the PCT.

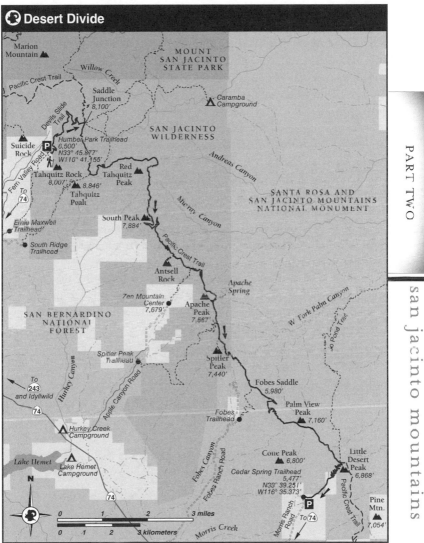

Marion Mountain ▲

MOUNT SAN JACINTO STATE PARK

Willow Creek

Pacific Crest Trail

Saddle Junction 8,100'

Devils Slide Trail

▲ Caramba Campground

SAN JACINTO WILDERNESS

Humber Park Trailhead 6,500' N33° 45.877' W116° 41.155'

Suicide Rock P

Fern Valley Road

Tahquitz Rock 8,007'

Red Tahquitz Peak ▲

8,846'

Tahquitz Peak

Andreas Canyon

SANTA ROSA AND SAN JACINTO MOUNTAINS NATIONAL MONUMENT

To (74)

Ernie Maxwell Trailhead

South Peak 7,884' ▲▲

Murray Canyon

South Ridge Trailhead

Pacific Crest Trail

Antsell Rock ▲

Apache Spring

Zen Mountain Center 7,679'

Apache Peak 7,567' ▲

W. Fork Palm Canyon

SAN BERNARDINO NATIONAL FOREST

Spitler Peak Trailhead

Hurkey Canyon

Spitler Peak 7,440' ▲

Fobes Saddle 5,980'

Palm View Peak ▲ 7,160'

To (243) and Idyllwild

(74)

Apple Canyon Road

Fobes Trailhead

Hurkey Creek Campground

Cone Peak ▲ 6,800'

Little Desert Peak 6,868'

Lake Hemet

Lake Hemet Campground

N

Fobes Canyon

Fobes Ranch Road

Cedar Spring Trailhead 5,477' N33° 39.251' W116° 35.373'

Pacific Crest Trail

Pine Mtn. ▲ 7,054'

(74)

P

Morris Ranch Road

To (74)

0   1   2   3 miles

0   1   2   3 kilometers

Morris Creek

The southbound PCT briefly leads east, north, and east again to bypass the stone battlements of Red Tahquitz Peak. In 0.8 mile, pass a trail leading north to Little Tahquitz Valley, but stay on the PCT as it leads east around a knob overlooking Andreas Canyon and south across the head of Murray Canyon. You are now properly on the Desert Divide. This highest and most rugged section is crowned with Jeffrey pines, white firs, and incense cedars.

In 3.2 miles, pass the eastern side of South Peak and turn west across the south flank. Look for a climber's trail, possibly marked with a cairn, leading 0.1 mile up to the nearby summit. The PCT switchbacks as it descends toward hulking Antsell Rock ahead. The trail bypasses the cliffs by dropping far down on the east side. In 2.1 miles, look for a cairn at the base of a gully in a grove of black oaks. From here, a strenuous climber's trail and a rock scramble lead to Antsell's massive granite summit, the most difficult and thrilling mountain along the divide (see Hike 9, page 53).

The PCT continues south to a saddle. In 0.5 mile, pass an unmarked trail on the right leading down to the Zen Mountain Center in Apple Canyon. Hike past the red battlements on the

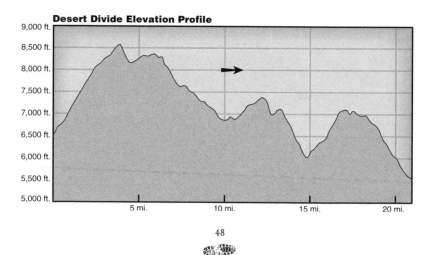

Desert Divide Elevation Profile

Aerial view of the Desert Divide from the south

Desert Divide from the east

north wall of Apache Peak. The 2008 Apache Fire, caused by a careless smoker, scorched the east side of the divide in this area. In 0.4 mile, pass a short spur to a vista just before rounding the corner. Cross another burn zone and loop around to Apache Peak's summit plateau in 1.2 miles. A short detour leads to the unimposing peak, which offers terrific views.

After continuing south on the PCT for 0.1 mile, reach a signed junction on the left with the trail to Apache Spring. This trail drops 500 feet in 0.5 mile to reach the reliable Apache Spring, where some small clearings offer your best bet for camping along the Desert Divide. The Forest Service recommends treating the springwater before drinking it.

The PCT leads south for 0.6 mile to a junction with Spitler Peak Trail coming up from Apple Canyon. It then climbs along the east side of Spitler Peak. A climber's trail at the north end of the peak offers access to the brushy summit.

South Peak   Red Tahquitz Peak   San Jacinto

South of Spitler Peak, the divide loses its rugged character. The peaks become lower and more rounded, and the subalpine conifer forest gives way to oak, manzanita, buckthorn, and ribbonwood. In 2.0 miles, reach Fobes Saddle, where a trail comes up from Fobes Canyon (an alternative exit point if you'd prefer a shorter trip). The PCT makes a long switchback, crosses to the west side of the divide, and climbs 2.3 miles to a flattish area, Palm View Peak. The true summit is hidden in a dense grove of oaks and firs 0.2 mile to the east and, having neither palms nor views, offers little appeal.

Continue southeast over rolling hills and along a boulevard cut through the manzanita to reach Cedar Spring Trail junction in 1.4 miles. Turn right onto Cedar Spring Trail and descend off the divide. In 1.3 miles, pass a gate and reach a picnic bench. The trail briefly follows a dirt road, then veers off to the right and passes several more gates between fenced properties to arrive at your vehicle in 1.0 mile.

DIRECTIONS   This trip requires a 19-mile car shuttle between Cedar Spring and Humber Park Trailheads.

Arrange for a vehicle at Cedar Spring Trailhead at the southern end of the trip. From Highway 74 8.6 miles southeast of Mountain Center in Garner Valley just south of mile marker 074 RIV 67.75, turn left (northeast) onto Morris Ranch Rd. (6S53). Proceed 3.7 miles to Cedar Spring Trailhead on the right. If you reach Morris Ranch, you've gone 0.25 mile too far. Trailhead parking is limited, but there's plenty of parking on the road 0.1 mile south of the trailhead.

Return to Highway 74. Turn right and drive north to Mountain Center, then make a right onto Highway 243 and continue north 4.5 miles to Idyllwild. Just before reaching Idyllwild Ranger Station, turn northeast on North Circle Dr. (You may need to stop at the ranger station to pick up your wilderness permit.) Drive 0.7 mile to a four-way intersection and turn right on South Circle Dr. Make the first left onto Fern Valley Rd. Proceed 1.8 miles to large Humber Park Trailhead at the end of the road.

PERMIT   A Forest Adventure Pass is required to park at the trailhead. Campfires are prohibited. Groups are limited to 12 persons. A San Jacinto Wilderness permit is required for day and overnight travel. Obtain the wilderness permit in person or by mail up to 90 days in advance from the Idyllwild Ranger Station (see Appendix: Managing Agencies, page 177, or www.fsva.org).

The quota for day and overnight wilderness permits from Humber Park is routinely filled in advance during the peak summer hiking season. If Humber Park permits are unavailable, consider starting at the south end where usage is much lighter.

OTHER POINTS OF INTEREST   Idyllwild County Park has a good campground. A network of trails leading to Idyllwild Nature Center offers a pleasant afternoon excursion. Hurkey Creek County Park and Lake Hemet also have campgrounds. Free, secluded, first-come, first-served campsites can be found at numbered yellow posts on dirt Thomas Mountain Road.

9 Antsell Rock

SCENERY: ✿ ✿ ✿ ✿
CHILDREN: ✿ ✿
DIFFICULTY: ✿ ✿ ✿ ✿
SOLITUDE: ✿ ✿ ✿ ✿
DISTANCE: *4 miles (out-and-back)*
ELEVATION GAIN: *2,300'*
HIKING TIME: *4 hours*

BEST TIMES: *April–June, October–November*
RECOMMENDED MAP: Santa Rosa and
San Jacinto Mountains National Monument
TOM HARRISON MAP: San Jacinto Wilderness
USFS PCT MAP: Volume 1
OUTSTANDING FEATURES: *Rock scrambling*

Antsell Rock is the most dramatic of the granite summits protruding from the Desert Divide south of Tahquitz Peak. The rock was named by Edmund Perkins of the U.S. Geological Survey for an artist at the Keen Camp Resort who was painting the peak. This hike follows the PCT to the back side of the mountain and then makes a short but very steep cross-country climb to the 7,679-foot summit. The final portion of the ascent requires scrambling on steep rocks; this trip is not for those fearful of heights or unsure of their step.

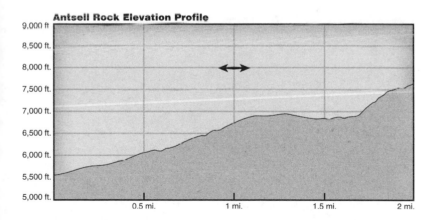

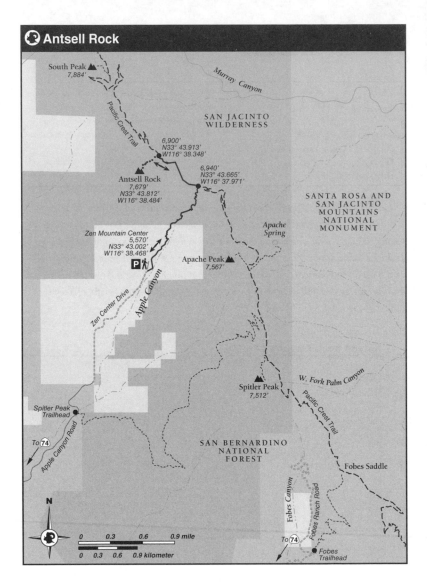

Antsell Rock

South Peak
7,884'

Murray Canyon

Pacific Crest Trail

SAN JACINTO
WILDERNESS

6,900'
N33° 43.913'
W116° 38.348'

6,940'
N33° 43.665'
W116° 37.971'

Antsell Rock
7,679'
N33° 43.812'
W116° 38.484'

SANTA ROSA AND
SAN JACINTO
MOUNTAINS
NATIONAL
MONUMENT

Apache
Spring

Zen Mountain Center
5,570'
N33° 43.002'
W116° 38.468'

P

Apache Peak
7,567'

Zen Center Drive

Apple Canyon

W. Fork Palm Canyon

Spitler Peak
7,512'

Pacific Crest Trail

Spitler Peak
Trailhead

To 74

Apple Canyon Road

SAN BERNARDINO
NATIONAL
FOREST

Fobes Saddle

Fobes Canyon

Fobes Ranch Road

N

0   0.3   0.6   0.9 mile

0   0.3   0.6   0.9 kilometer

To 74

Fobes
Trailhead

54

Antsell Rock

This trail begins on private land owned by the Zen Mountain Center. The center graciously permits hikers to cross their property; please protect this privilege for future hikers by keeping your group small and your voices quiet and by not bringing dogs.

🚶🚶 Walk up the dirt road through the Zen Center gate. Stay left at a fork by the office, and then left again at a fork near the cabins. In 0.3 mile, reach an unsigned trail by two water tanks at a switchback in the road. Follow the beautiful trail up the canyon along a seasonal creek beneath incense cedars, Coulter pines, and black oaks. Pass a spur leading to the creek and reach the crest in 0.9 mile.

Turn left (west) and follow the PCT around the northeast side of Antsell Rock. In 0.5 mile, watch for a gully marked with cairns in a grove of black oaks. A steep and loose climber's trail ascends this gully to a prominent notch on the right side of the rocky peak. The summit register is found in the notch.

This notch is a good turnaround point for those uneasy with rock scrambling. Mountaineers will enjoy scrambling up a weakness in the rock above the notch, going left around a corner, and following another tree-filled gully to the rocky summit ridge.

DIRECTIONS   From Highway 74 3.4 miles southeast of Mountain Center and just south of mile marker 074 RIV 62.75, turn left (east) onto Apple Canyon Rd. Proceed 3.3 miles to its end at Pine Springs Ranch. Immediately before entering the ranch, veer right onto a private dirt road leading to the Zen Mountain Center. Park at a small dirt lot on the left in 1.1 miles, just before entering the center.

PERMIT   A San Jacinto Wilderness permit is required. Groups are limited to 12 persons. Obtain the wilderness permit in person or by mail up to 90 days in advance from the Idyllwild Ranger Station (see Appendix: Managing Agencies, page 177, or www.fsva.org).

OTHER POINTS OF INTEREST   Campgrounds can be found at Hurkey Creek County Park and Lake Hemet. Hurkey Creek is also famous for its mountain bike races. Free, secluded, first-come, first-served campsites can be found at numbered yellow posts on dirt Thomas Mountain Road.

10 Tahquitz Peak

SCENERY: ☆ ☆ ☆ ☆	HIKING TIME: *5 hours or 2 days*
CHILDREN: ☆ ☆	BEST TIMES: *May–November*
DIFFICULTY: ☆ ☆ ☆	RECOMMENDED MAP: Santa Rosa and
SOLITUDE: ☆ ☆	San Jacinto Mountains National Monument
DISTANCE: *9 miles (out-and-back)*	TOM HARRISON MAP: San Jacinto Wilderness
or 11 miles (loop)	USFS PCT MAP: Volume 1
ELEVATION GAIN: *2,400'*	OUTSTANDING FEATURES: *Views*

Tahquitz Peak is a massive granite summit overlooking the quiet town of Idyllwild. This hike to the summit is one of the most popular in the region. Backpackers have the option of camping in the lovely forest near the peak. Hikers mispronounce the name in a variety of ways, but the Cahuilla Indians say "TAW-kwish" in memory of their legendary soul-eating shaman who is reputed to still haunt the mountain.

🥾🥾 From Humber Park, hike up Devil's Slide Trail 2.5 miles to Saddle Junction. This steep ascent was once the bane of cattle ranchers, whose cows made the treacherous climb over thorn bushes, fallen

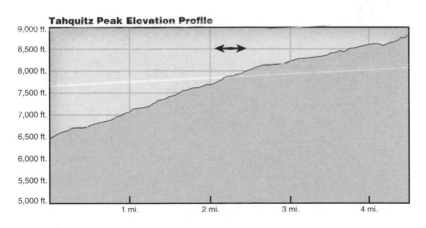

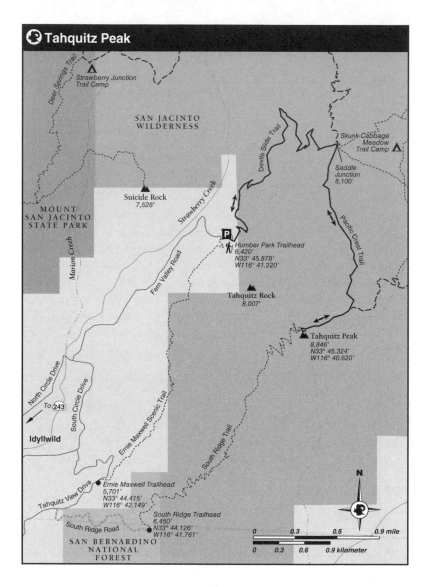

Tahquitz Peak

Deer Springs Trail

Strawberry Junction
Trail Camp

SAN JACINTO
WILDERNESS

Skunk-Cabbage
Meadow
Trail Camp

Devils Slide Trail

Saddle
Junction
8,100'

Suicide Rock
7,528'

MOUNT
SAN JACINTO
STATE PARK

Marion Creek

Strawberry Creek

Pacific Crest Trail

P

Humber Park Trailhead
6,420'
N33° 45.878'
W116° 41.220'

Fern Valley Road

Tahquitz Rock
8,007'

Tahquitz Peak
8,846'
N33° 45.324'
W116° 40.620'

North Circle Drive

South Circle Drive

To 243

Ernie Maxwell Scenic Trail

South Ridge Trail

Idyllwild

N

Tahquitz View Drive

Ernie Maxwell Trailhead
5,701'
N33° 44.415'
W116° 42.149'

South Ridge Road

South Ridge Trailhead
6,450'
N33° 44.126'
W116° 41.761'

SAN BERNARDINO
NATIONAL
FOREST

| 0 | 0.3 | 0.6 | 0.9 mile |
| 0 | 0.3 | 0.6 | 0.9 kilometer |

Tahquitz Peak Fire Lookout

logs, and loose boulders to reach summer pastures in Tahquitz Valley. The trail is now so well-built that some have renamed it Angels Glide, but the ascent is still strenuous. The trail offers fine views of Suicide Rock across Strawberry Valley and of Yosemite-like Tahquitz Rock nearby. These Southern California landmarks echo with the calls of rock climbers whenever the weather is favorable.

At the five-way junction, backpackers have the option of continuing east to reach good camping in Skunk Cabbage Meadow or Tahquitz Valley. However, day hikers make a hard right and head south on the PCT. As you climb, the trees become smaller and more weather-beaten. In 1.4 miles, reach a junction with South Ridge Trail. Turn right and follow it for 0.4 mile, then take a short spur to the 8,846-foot summit of Tahquitz Peak.

The Tahquitz Peak Fire Lookout atop the peak is staffed by fire spotters from the San Bernardino National Forest Association during fire season. These friendly volunteers are happy to point out the sights and share their knowledge about the San Jacinto Mountains.

Return the way you came. Or, for a terrific 11-mile loop, descend South Ridge Trail 3.5 miles to South Ridge Road. Follow the road west and then north for 0.9 mile; then turn right on Tahquitz View Dr. and walk 0.2 mile to Ernie Maxwell Scenic Trail, which leads 2.5 miles back north to Humber Park.

DIRECTIONS   From Highway 243 just south of the Idyllwild Ranger Station, turn northeast on North Circle Dr. (You may need to stop at the ranger station to pick up your wilderness permit.) Drive 0.7 mile to a four-way intersection and turn right on South Circle Dr. Make the first left onto Fern Valley Rd. Proceed 1.8 miles to large Humber Park Trailhead at the end of the road.

PERMIT   A Forest Adventure Pass is required. Campfires are prohibited. Groups are limited to 12 persons. A San Jacinto Wilderness permit is required for day and overnight travel. Obtain the wilderness permit in person or by mail up to 90 days in advance from the Idyllwild Ranger Station (see Appendix: Managing Agencies, page 177, or www.fsva.org).

The quota for day and overnight wilderness permits from Humber Park is routinely filled in advance during the peak summer hiking season. If Humber Park permits are unavailable, a good alternative is to start at South Ridge Trailhead instead.

OTHER POINTS OF INTEREST   Idyllwild County Park has a good campground. A network of trails leading to Idyllwild Nature Center offers a pleasant afternoon excursion.

11 San Jacinto Loop from Idyllwild

SCENERY: ✿ ✿ ✿ ✿ ✿	BEST TIMES: *May–October*
CHILDREN: ✿	RECOMMENDED MAP: Santa Rosa and
DIFFICULTY: ✿ ✿ ✿ ✿ ✿	San Jacinto Mountains National Monument
SOLITUDE: ✿ ✿	TOM HARRISON MAP: San Jacinto Wilderness
DISTANCE: *20 miles (loop)*	USFS PCT MAP: Volume I
ELEVATION GAIN: *4,500'*	OUTSTANDING FEATURES: *Grand circuit of*
HIKING TIME: *11 hours or 2–3 days*	*San Jacinto*

San Jacinto Peak, at 10,834 feet, is the northern culmination of the Peninsular Ranges that extend all the way from Baja California. This loop provides a gorgeous tour of the San Jacinto Wilderness high country and is my personal favorite hike on the mountain. Most of the hike traverses a lovely landscape of open forest and granite boulders above 8,000 feet in elevation. The trip can be done as a long day hike or as a backpacking trip with several fine campsites along the way. Backpackers should be aware that water becomes harder to find as the summer progresses; ask about current conditions at the Idyllwild Ranger Station.

🏃🏃 From Humber Park, lumber up the unrelenting Devil's Slide Trail to reach the PCT at Saddle Junction in 2.5 miles. The trail offers fine views of Suicide Rock across Strawberry Valley and of Yosemite-like Tahquitz Rock nearby. These Southern California landmarks echo with the calls of rock climbers whenever the weather is favorable. Good camping and water is available near Saddle Junction at Skunk Cabbage Meadow and Tahquitz Valley if you are looking for a short first day.

Turn sharply left and follow the northbound PCT 1.9 miles up the ridge above Strawberry Valley. At the next junction, stay on the PCT as it turns left and cuts across the chaparral-clad north wall of the valley. The views of Tahquitz and Suicide Rocks are particularly good. Cross Strawberry Creek, which flows from its source high on Marion Mountain. You may be able to refill water here, although the

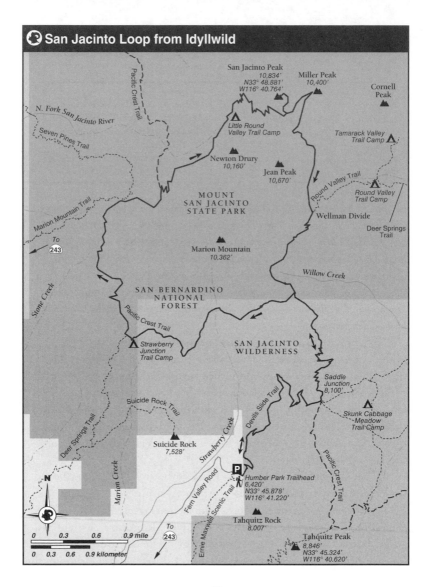

San Jacinto Loop from Idyllwild

Pacific Crest Trail

San Jacinto Peak
10,834'
N33° 48.881'
W116° 40.764'

Miller Peak
10,400'

Cornell
Peak

N. Fork San Jacinto River

Seven Pines Trail

Little Round
Valley Trail Camp

Tamarack Valley
Trail Camp

Newton Drury
10,160'

Jean Peak
10,670'

Round Valley Trail

Round Valley
Trail Camp

Marion Mountain Trail

MOUNT
SAN JACINTO
STATE PARK

Wellman Divide

Deer Springs
Trail

To
243

Marion Mountain
10,362'

Stone Creek

Willow Creek

SAN BERNARDINO
NATIONAL
FOREST

Pacific Crest Trail

SAN JACINTO
WILDERNESS

Strawberry
Junction
Trail Camp

Saddle
Junction
8,100'

Suicide Rock Trail

Devils Slide Trail

Skunk Cabbage
Meadow
Trail Camp

Deer Springs Trail

Suicide Rock
7,528'

Marion Creek

Strawberry Creek

Pacific Crest Trail

P

Humber Park Trailhead
6,420'
N33° 45.878'
W116° 41.220'

N

Fern Valley Road

Ernie Maxwell Scenic Trail

To
243

Tahquitz Rock
8,007'

Tahquitz Peak
8,846'
N33° 45.324'
W116° 40.620'

0   0.3   0.6   0.9 mile

0   0.3   0.6   0.9 kilometer

creek is dry by late summer. In 2.2 miles, reach the dry but beautifully situated Strawberry Junction Trail Camp shaded by tall Jeffrey pines. A junction with Deer Springs Trail is just beyond.

Turn right (north) at the junction to stay on the PCT. The open forest of Jeffrey pines and white firs is one of the most enchanting in Southern California. In 2.3 miles, pass consecutive junctions with the Marion Mountain and Seven Pines Trails. In another 0.5 mile, reach a junction with the Little Round Valley Trail marking the end of your journey on the PCT.

Turn right and climb 1.0 mile to Little Round Valley, where excellent camping can be found near the seasonal stream. Continue 1.3 miles to a saddle south of San Jacinto Peak. To reach the peak, turn left and hike north for 0.3 mile, passing a stone emergency shelter, to scale the granite summit boulders. San Jacinto Peak's summit is the second highest in Southern California and offers unrivaled views. *Camping is prohibited at the summit.*

Return to the saddle and descend on the east side of the mountain. The prominent pyramid to the east is Cornell Peak. The trail makes a long switchback to the north before turning south and

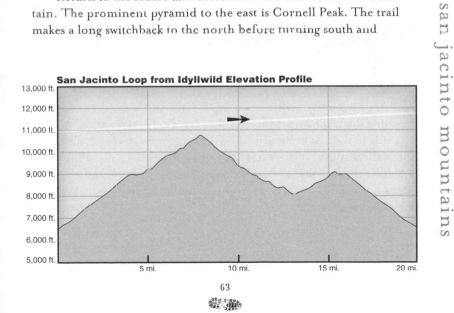

San Jacinto Loop from Idyllwild Elevation Profile

Suicide Rock and sugar pine

reaching the Wellman Divide in 2.4 miles. Backpackers may detour
1.0 mile to the east to Round Valley Campground, a crowded site
with reliable piped springwater. But this trip continues south for
1.2 miles, passing the swampy Wellman Cienega, to rejoin the PCT.
Retrace the initial segment of your trip down to Saddle Junction and
Humber Park.

DIRECTIONS   From Highway 243 just south of the Idyllwild Ranger Station, turn northeast on North Circle Dr. (You may need to stop at the ranger station to pick up your wilderness permit.) Drive 0.7 mile to a four-way intersection, and turn right on South Circle Dr. Make the first left onto Fern Valley Rd. Proceed 1.8 miles to large Humber Park Trailhead at the end of the road.

PERMIT   A Forest Adventure Pass is required. Campfires and dogs are prohibited. Groups are limited to 12 persons. A San Jacinto Wilderness permit is required for day and overnight travel. Obtain the wilderness permit in person or by mail up to 90 days in advance from the Idyllwild Ranger Station (see Appendix: Managing Agencies, page 177, or www.fsva.org).

The quota for day and overnight wilderness permits from Humber Park is routinely filled a month in advance during the peak summer hiking season. If Humber Park permits are unavailable, good alternatives include Deer Springs or Marion Mountain Trailheads.

To camp at Strawberry Junction, Little Round Valley, or Round Valley, you must get an additional wilderness camping permit from the Mt. San Jacinto State Park. This permit costs $5 per person and can be obtained up to eight weeks in advance in person or by mail from the state park headquarters at: P.O. Box 308, 25905 Highway 243, Idyllwild, CA 92549, (951) 659-2607. Learn more at www.parks.ca.gov/pages/636/files/dpr409.pdf.

OTHER POINTS OF INTEREST   Idyllwild County Park has a good campground. A network of trails leading to Idyllwild Nature Center offers a pleasant afternoon excursion.

san jacinto mountains

12 San Jacinto via Fuller Ridge

SCENERY: ✿ ✿ ✿ ✿ ✿	BEST TIMES: *June–October*
CHILDREN: ✿	RECOMMENDED MAP: Santa Rosa and
DIFFICULTY: ✿ ✿ ✿ ✿	San Jacinto Mountains National Monument
SOLITUDE: ✿ ✿ ✿	TOM HARRISON MAP: San Jacinto Wilderness
DISTANCE: *15 miles (out–and–back)*	USFS PCT MAP: Volume I
ELEVATION GAIN: *4,100'*	OUTSTANDING FEATURES: *Rugged ridge and*
HIKING TIME: *8 hours or 2 days*	*high peak*

Fuller Ridge Trail starts high on the rugged northwest slope of San Jacinto. Although this trailhead might seem to offer easy access to the summit, the difficult terrain forces the trail to follow a circuitous path that adds both distance and elevation, resulting in a strenuous but rewarding trip. Although infamous among PCT thru–hikers who brave the icy ridge and precipitous drops in April, this section presents no undue difficulties by June when the snow has melted. Backpackers have the option of a pleasant stay at Little Round Valley Trail Camp just below the summit.

🚶🚶 Hike southeast on the PCT through a lush forest of sugar pines and white firs. In 1.0 mile, pass a saddle on the right, and cross

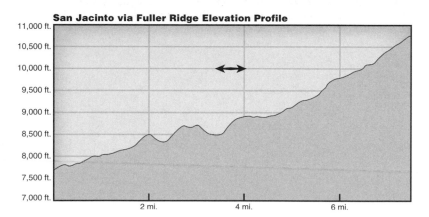

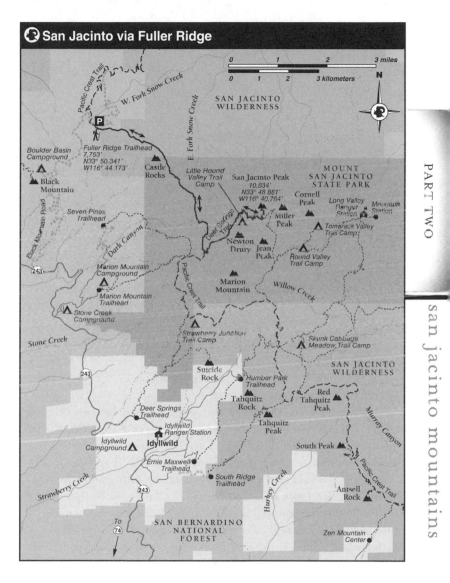

San Jacinto via Fuller Ridge

0   1   2   3 miles

0   1   2   3 kilometers

N

SAN JACINTO
WILDERNESS

Pacific Crest Trail

W. Fork Snow Creek

E. Fork Snow Creek

Boulder Basin
Campground

Black
Mountain

Fuller Ridge Trailhead
7,753'
N33° 50.341'
W116° 44.173'

Castle
Rocks

Little Round
Valley Trail Camp

San Jacinto Peak
10,834'
N33° 48.881'
W116° 40.764'

MOUNT
SAN JACINTO
STATE PARK

Cornell
Peak

Long Valley
Ranger
Station

Mountain
Station

Seven Pines
Trailhead

Deer Springs Trail

Miller
Peak

Tamarack Valley
Trail Camp

Black Mountain Road

Dark Canyon

Newton
Drury   Jean
Peak

Round Valley
Trail Camp

243

Marion Mountain
Campground

Marion Mountain
Trailhead

Pacific Crest Trail

Marion
Mountain

Willow Creek

Stone Creek
Campground

Stone Creek

Strawberry Junction
Trail Camp

Skunk Cabbage
Meadow Trail Camp

SAN JACINTO
WILDERNESS

243

Suicide
Rock

Humber Park
Trailhead

Tahquitz
Rock

Red
Tahquitz
Peak

Murray Canyon

Deer Springs
Trailhead

Idyllwild
Ranger Station

Tahquitz
Peak

Idyllwild
Campground   Idyllwild

South Peak

Pacific Crest Trail

Ernie Maxwell
Trailhead

Strawberry Creek

243

South Ridge
Trailhead

Hurkey Creek

Antsell
Rock

To
74

SAN BERNARDINO
NATIONAL
FOREST

Zen Mountain
Center

Fuller Ridge from Black Mountain

a huge field of wild blue and red currants, where you can enjoy a tasty snack in late summer. In 0.3 mile, cross the boundary into San Jacinto State Park.

In another 0.3 mile, begin switchbacking up steeply beneath the spires of Castle Rocks until you reach a saddle on the ridge. Enjoy the breathtaking views of Snow Creek on San Jacinto's awesome north face as the trail weaves around gendarmes on the rugged Fuller Ridge. Then contour south beneath Folly Peak across the headwaters of the San Jacinto River to meet Deer Springs Trail, 5 miles from the start.

Leaving the PCT, turn left (northeast) and follow Deer Springs Trail 1.0 mile to Little Round Valley Trail Camp located in a splendid bowl beside the seasonal creek. Continue 1.3 miles to a saddle south of San Jacinto Peak. To reach the peak, turn left and hike north for 0.3 mile, passing a stone emergency shelter before scaling the granite summit boulders. San Jacinto Peak's 10,834-foot summit is the second highest in Southern California and offers unrivaled views. *Camping is prohibited at the summit.*

DIRECTIONS   From Highway 243 0.5 mile south of mile marker 243 RIV 13.00, turn northeast up graded dirt Black Mtn. Rd. (4S01). Proceed 7.3 miles, passing side roads for Black Mtn. Campground and Black Mtn. Group Camp to a sign for Fuller Ridge Trailhead. Turn right and go 0.2 mile up the hill to park in a clearing.

PERMIT   A Forest Adventure Pass is required. Campfires and dogs are prohibited. Groups are limited to 15 persons. Mount San Jacinto State Wilderness permit required for day and overnight travel. This permit costs $5 per person; you can obtain it up to eight weeks in advance in person or by mail from the state park headquarters at: P.O. Box 308, 25905 Highway 243, Idyllwild, CA 92549, (951) 659-2607. Learn more at www.parks.ca.gov/pages/636/files/dpr409.pdf.

OTHER POINTS OF INTEREST   Black Mountain Campground has attractive campsites. If you arrive a day ahead of your trip, the Black Mountain Fire Lookout is within walking distance of the campground and offers panoramic views of Fuller Ridge.

San Bernardino Mountains

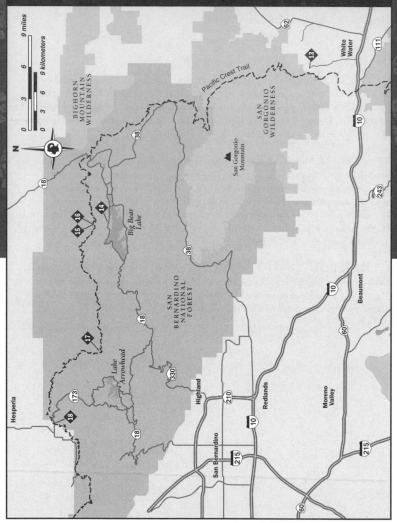

3

SAN BERNARDINO
MOUNTAINS

SCENERY: ☆ ☆ ☆ ☆	ELEVATION GAIN: *800'*
CHILDREN: ☆ ☆	HIKING TIME: *4 hours*
DIFFICULTY: ☆ ☆ ☆	BEST TIMES: *October–April*
SOLITUDE: ☆ ☆ ☆	USFS PCT MAP: Volume 1
DISTANCE: *8 miles (one-way with shuttle)*	OUTSTANDING FEATURES: *Rivers in the desert*

Whitewater River, a desert river fed by the snows of San Gorgonio, is a new favorite among Southern California hikers. The PCT follows the river up Whitewater Canyon and over a divide into Mission Creek Canyon. Whitewater Canyon was once privately held, but the Wildlands Conservancy now operates a hiker–friendly visitor center at Whitewater Canyon. The best time to go is in the spring, when the river runs strong and the wildflowers are in bloom. Families enjoy walking the first mile of the trail and playing along the river, but watch children closely during times of high flow.

🚶🚶 Sign in at the ranger station or trailhead register. From the signed trailhead on the north side of the parking lot, hike north between a pair of palm trees. Follow the rock-lined trail as it briefly merges with a dirt road before turning west and crossing the wash. Regular flooding makes it difficult to define a trail through the wash, but posts will help you navigate. Join the Pacific Crest Trail at a signed junction near the west wall of the canyon, 0.6 mile from the trailhead. Follow the PCT north for 1.4 miles past desert willows and brittle bushes to a small volcanic knob called Red Dome.

The PCT crosses Whitewater River wash here. Look north-northeast to pick out the closest canyon. Occasional posts and PCT trail markers may help you find your route, and logs or rocks may help you cross the river. The PCT resumes at the far northwestern edge of the canyon in 0.4 mile. It passes desert vegetation including cactus, mesquite, and Mojave yucca, then switchbacks to reach an abrupt saddle at the head of the canyon in 0.7 mile. This portion of the trip

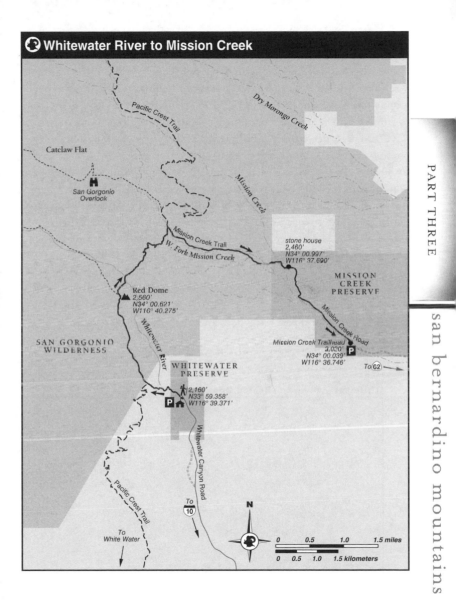

Whitewater River to Mission Creek

Pacific Crest Trail

Dry Morongo Creek

Catclaw Flat

San Gorgonio Overlook

Mission Creek

Mission Creek Trail

W. Fork Mission Creek

stone house
2,460'
N34° 00.997'
W116° 37.690'

Red Dome
2,560'
N34° 00.621'
W116° 40.275'

MISSION
CREEK
PRESERVE

SAN GORGONIO
WILDERNESS

Whitewater River

Mission Creek Road

Mission Creek Trailhead
2,020'
N34° 00.039'
W116° 36.746'

To 62

WHITEWATER
PRESERVE

2,160'
N33° 59.358'
W116° 39.371'

Whitewater Canyon Road

Pacific Crest Trail

To
10

To
White Water

N

0   0.5   1.0   1.5 miles

0   0.5   1.0   1.5 kilometers

offers great views of San Jacinto, whose north face is cut by dramatic Snow Creek. Descend 0.6 mile to the floor of Mission Creek's West Fork, where you'll find the signed Mission Creek Trail on the right.

The Wildlands Conservancy has recently done trail work to repair the path that was chewed up by bulldozers during the 2006 Sawtooth Complex Fire. Triggered by summer lightning, the fire burned 61,000 acres, destroyed 50 homes, and killed one civilian. The sedimentary rocks in this area are beautifully tinted green, purple, brown, and white. In 1.9 miles, reach the junction with another canyon coming in from the left. Hike east across the North Fork of Mission Creek. The trail may disappear in the wide wash but resumes at a trail marker on the far side. In another 0.2 mile, reach Stone House in Mission Creek Preserve, where you'll find shaded picnicking. Camping is available with permission in advance from the Wildlands Conservancy.

Walk southeast down the good dirt road to exit the preserve. Watch for Painted Hills Wetlands where wild grapevines thrive beneath an ancient cottonwood. In 1.6 miles, pass the ruins of T Cross K Ranch and reach the gate and parking area for Mission Creek Preserve.

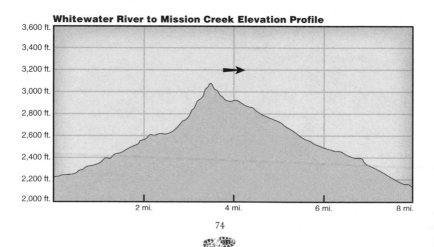

74

Crossing Whitewater River

DIRECTIONS   This trip requires a 15-mile car shuttle between Mission Creek Preserve and Whitewater Canyon Preserve. If a shuttle is *not* available, an alternative is to make a 4-mile out-and-back trip from Whitewater Canyon to Red Dome.

Arrange for a vehicle at the Mission Creek Preserve. From Interstate 10, exit north on Highway 62. In 5 miles, at mile marker 062 RIV 05.00, turn left onto the graded dirt Mission Creek Rd. at an easy-to-miss sign. Proceed 2.3 miles, staying left at a fork, to a gate at the preserve boundary.

Return to Interstate 10 and drive west, then make the first exit north onto Whitewater Canyon Rd. Follow the frontage road that veers east, then turn left onto Whitewater Canyon Rd. Proceed 4.9 miles to the end of the road at the large parking area for Whitewater Preserve.

PERMIT   Hikers are required to sign in at the ranger station or trailhead register. Whitewater Preserve is open daily from 8 a.m. to 5 p.m. except on Thanksgiving, Christmas, and New Year's Day and during dangerous weather.

OTHER POINTS OF INTEREST   Free camping is available if you get permission in advance at Whitewater Preserve Ranger Station and at the stone house in Mission Creek Preserve.

14 Cougar Crest

SCENERY: ✿ ✿ ✿	HIKING TIME: *2 hours*
CHILDREN: ✿ ✿ ✿	BEST TIMES: *April—November*
DIFFICULTY: ✿ ✿	USFS PCT MAP: Volume 2
SOLITUDE: ✿	OUTSTANDING FEATURES: *Walk in the woods*
DISTANCE: *5 miles (out-and-back)*	*above Big Bear Lake.*
ELEVATION GAIN: *700'*	

Cougar Crest Trail is technically a hike to the PCT rather than a hike on the PCT, but it is a very popular, accessible trip enjoyed by numerous Big Bear visitors. The trail climbs lush forested slopes to join the PCT on the ridge between Big Bear Lake and Holcomb Valley.

🚶🚶 From the large and well-marked trailhead parking area, walk north on paved Alpine Pedal Path for 0.1 mile. At a signed junction where the paved path turns right and heads toward Big Bear Discovery Center, continue straight onto dirt Cougar Crest Trail (1E22). The forest of Jeffrey pines, incense cedars, and western junipers is particularly beautiful in this area.

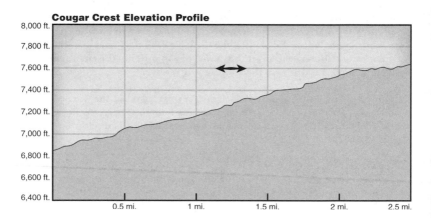

Cougar Crest Elevation Profile

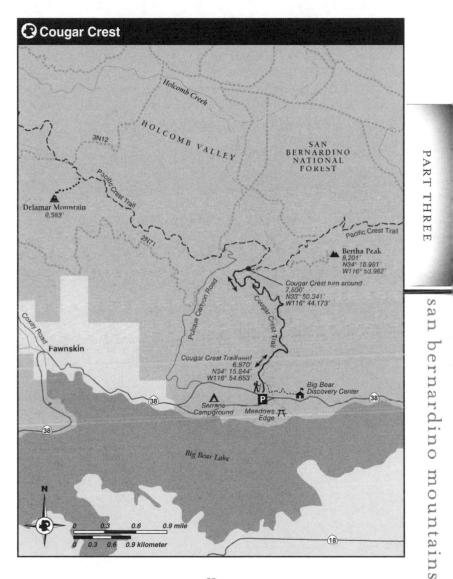

Cougar Crest

Holcomb Creek

HOLCOMB VALLEY

3N12

SAN
BERNARDINO
NATIONAL
FOREST

Pacific Crest Trail

Delamar Mountain
8,383'

2N71

Pacific Crest Trail

Bertha Peak
8,201'
N34° 16.981'
W116° 53.962'

Cougar Crest turn around
7,590'
N33° 50.341'
W116° 44.173'

Palique Canyon Road

Cougar Crest Trail

Coxey Road

Fawnskin

Cougar Crest Trailhead
6,870'
N34° 15.844'
W116° 54.653'

Big Bear
Discovery Center

38

38

Serrano
Campground

Meadows
Edge

38

Big Bear Lake

N

0   0.3   0.6   0.9 mile

0   0.3   0.6   0.9 kilometer

18

After 2 miles of moderate but sustained climbing, shortly before reaching the crest, your best views of Big Bear Lake open up behind you. Also, look for the fire lookout perched atop Butler Peak to the west. The rest of the peak was incinerated during the 2007 Butler II Fire, triggered by lightning and rekindled by strong winds after firefighters believed it was under control. Cross the crest and turn east for 0.3 mile to reach the junction with the PCT near a magnificent stand of pinyon pines.

From the junction, it is possible to turn either direction and follow the PCT. However, the dense forest limits the view. Most hikers simply enjoy a snack and retrace their steps back down.

DIRECTIONS   Park at Cougar Crest Trailhead on Highway 38 near mile marker 038 SBD 53.50. The trailhead is on the north shore of Big Bear Lake a half mile west of Big Bear Discovery Center.

PERMIT   Forest Adventure Pass required.

OTHER POINTS OF INTEREST   Big Bear Lake is a popular resort area with many options for boating, mountain biking, hiking, rock climbing, dining, and lodging. Serrano Campground on Highway 38 is conveniently located for this trip.

15 Delamar Mountain

SCENERY: ✿ ✿ ✿
CHILDREN: ✿ ✿ ✿
DIFFICULTY: ✿ ✿
SOLITUDE: ✿ ✿ ✿ ✿
DISTANCE: *5 miles (out-and-back)*
ELEVATION GAIN: *800'*

HIKING TIME: *3 hours*
BEST TIMES: *April–November*
USFS PCT MAP: Volume 2
OUTSTANDING FEATURES: *Lake views from the summit*

At 8,398 feet, Delamar Mountain is the highest point on the ridge between Big Bear Lake and Holcomb Valley. Its boulder-covered summit stands above the forest, providing panoramic views of the San Bernardino Mountains. This hike reaches the summit by following the PCT through the forest, then making a steep cross-country ascent of the mountain's north slopes.

🚶🚶 This trip starts where the PCT crosses Polique Canyon Rd. The eastern side is well-marked with a sign for the Holcomb View Trail, but your hike begins on the lesser-marked west side. The trail

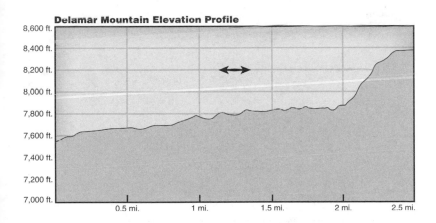

Delamar Mountain Elevation Profile

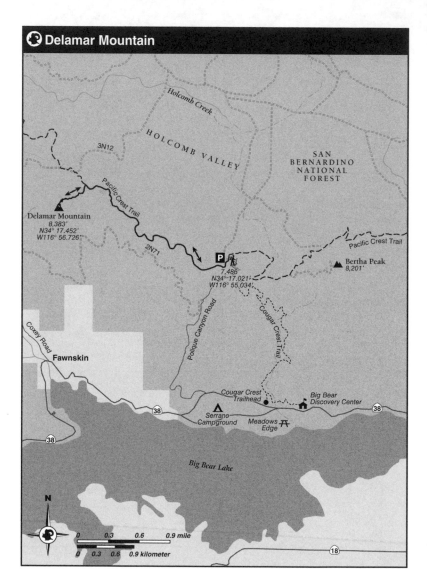

Delamar Mountain

Holcomb Creek

HOLCOMB VALLEY

3N12

SAN
BERNARDINO
NATIONAL
FOREST

Pacific Crest Trail

Delamar Mountain
8,383'
N34° 17.452'
W116° 56.726'

Pacific Crest Trail

2N71

Bertha Peak
8,201'

P

7,486'
N34° 17.021'
W116° 55.034'

Coxey Road

Polique Canyon Road

Cougar Crest Trail

Fawnskin

Cougar Crest
Trailhead

Big Bear
Discovery Center

38

Serrano
Campground

Meadows
Edge

38

38

Big Bear Lake

N

0   0.3   0.6   0.9 mile

0   0.3   0.6   0.9 kilometer

18

Big Bear Lake and San Gorgonio Mountain from Delamar Mountain

leads into a forest of Jeffrey pines and black oaks mixed with the occasional white fir and beautiful western juniper. Delamar Mountain's broad summit lies ahead, with the Butler Peak fire lookout perched on the scorched mountain behind. From time to time, clearings offer southward views of gemlike Big Bear Lake below, with San Gorgonio rearing its mighty 11,499-foot summit beyond. Big Bear Lake is a reservoir originally dammed in 1884 by the citrus ranchers of Redlands to supply dependable water for their groves.

In 1.4 miles, the trail crosses to the northern side of the ridge, where you can glimpse Holcomb Valley through the trees to the north. The valley is named for Bill Holcomb, a prospector who found gold in the area while hunting grizzly bears in 1859. Within two years, 1,400 people had flocked to the area seeking their fortunes, but they rapidly depleted the placer gold and abandoned the valley.

In another 0.8 mile, where the trail begins to descend after passing a ravine, arrive at a good spot to leave the trail and strike uphill for the mountaintop. There is no trail, but thread your own path northwestward through the trees for another steep 0.3 mile to reach the granite summit boulders. The vegetation is not too dense, so there are many other options for reaching the summit.

DIRECTIONS   From Highway 38 on the north shore of Big Bear Lake at mile marker 038 SBD 54.04, turn north onto the good dirt Polique Canyon Rd. (Forest Road 2N09). Proceed 2.3 miles to the top of the ridge, where you will see the signed Holcomb View Trail. Limited roadside parking is available just beyond.

PERMIT   Forest Adventure Pass required.

OTHER POINTS OF INTEREST   Big Bear Lake is a popular resort area with many options for boating, mountain biking, hiking, rock climbing, dining, and lodging. Serrano Campground on Highway 38 is conveniently located for this trip.

SCENERY: ✿ ✿ ✿ ✿	HIKING TIME: *2–4 days*
CHILDREN: ✿	BEST TIMES: *April–May, October–November*
DIFFICULTY: ✿ ✿ ✿ ✿	USFS PCT MAP: Volume 2
SOLITUDE: ✿ ✿ ✿ ✿	OUTSTANDING FEATURES: *Long backpack*
DISTANCE: *35 miles (one-way with shuttle)*	*following creeks through the San Bernardino*
ELEVATION GAIN: *2,000' (6,300' loss)*	*Mountains*

This trip is a big one, tracing a pair of delightful creeks down the length of the San Bernardino Mountains. Although it passes near some of Southern California's biggest mountain resorts and through areas frequented by ATVs, you'll generally feel like you are completely away from civilization. You'll gradually descend through the major ecosystems of the region, from mountain forests of pine, fir, and oak through chaparral and into the Mojave Desert, following the beautiful canyons of Holcomb and Deep Creeks. Three major wildfires have affected large segments of the trail since 1999, and you'll see both devastation and regeneration.

It is best done in spring or fall. The snow usually melts enough above Big Bear Lake to make the trail passable by mid-April. Call Big Bear Discovery Center for current conditions. During this early season, hikers enjoy dozens of seasonal creeks and plentiful wildflowers. However, Holcomb Creek can be challenging to ford if the logs and stones hikers use to cross are submerged. A pair of sandals facilitates the creek crossings. Also, the burned areas are prone to heavy deadfall after winter storms. In the fall, weather and trail conditions are most dependable, but water is mostly limited to the major creek crossings. Wear bright colors during fall hunting season. Avoid Deep Creek on a hot summer day, when the canyon becomes an oven.

This trip can be readily shortened by exiting at Splinters Cabin or starting at any of the dirt roads in the Holcomb Creek area. You can lengthen it by starting further east above Big Bear.

🚶 The hike begins atop a ridge overlooking Big Bear Lake where the combination PCT and Holcomb View Trail crosses Polique

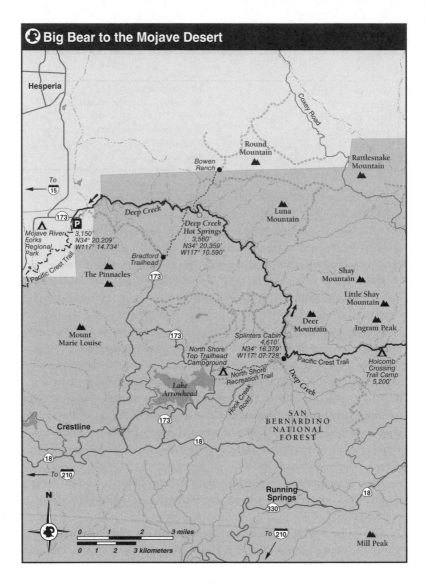

Hesperia

Coxey Road

Round
Mountain

Rattlesnake
Mountain

Bowen
Ranch

To
15

173

Deep Creek

Luna
Mountain

Mojave River
Forks
Regional
Park

3,150'
N34° 20.209'
W117° 14.734'

Deep Creek
Hot Springs
3,560'
N34° 20.359'
W117° 10.590'

Pacific Crest Trail

Bradford
Trailhead

The Pinnacles

173

Shay
Mountain

Little Shay
Mountain

Deer
Mountain

Ingram Peak

Mount
Marie Louise

173

Splinters Cabin
4,610'
N34° 16.379'
W117° 07.728'

North Shore
Top Trailhead
Campground

Pacific Crest Trail

Holcomb
Crossing
Trail Camp
5,200'

North Shore
Recreation Trail

Lake
Arrowhead

Hook Creek Road

Deep Creek

SAN
BERNARDINO
NATIONAL
FOREST

Crestline

173

18

18

To 210

18

N

Running
Springs

330

0   1   2   3 miles

0   1   2   3 kilometers

To 210

Mill Peak

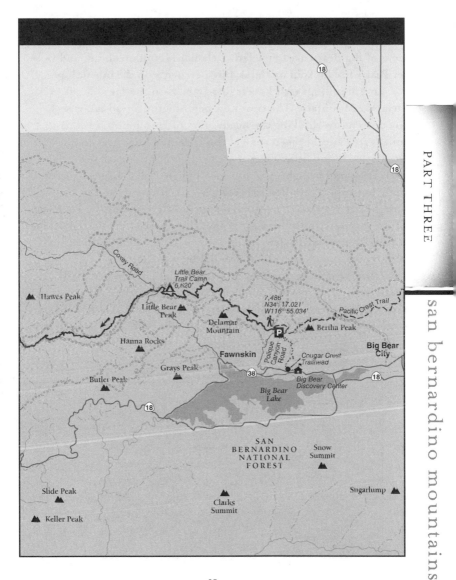

Hawes Peak

Coxey Road

Little Bear Trail Camp
6,620'

Little Bear Peak

7,486'
N34° 17.021'
W116° 55.034'

Delamar Mountain

Pacific Crest Trail

Bertha Peak

Hanna Rocks

Fawnskin

Polique Canyon Road

Big Bear City

Grays Peak

Cougar Crest Trailhead

Butler Peak

Big Bear Discovery Center

Big Bear Lake

SAN BERNARDINO NATIONAL FOREST

Snow Summit

Slide Peak

Sugarlump

Keller Peak

Clarks Summit

Canyon Rd. Signed Holcomb View Trail is on the east side of the road, but this trip follows the lesser-marked PCT on the west side. Look for views of Big Bear Lake to the left, Delamar Mountain ahead, and Butler Peak's fire lookout on the skyline perched atop the burnt slopes.

In 2.6 miles, reach Forest Road 3N12 on the far side of Delamar Mountain. The trail now begins a long gradual, weaving descent overlooking the headwaters of Holcomb Creek. In 0.7 mile, cross another jeep road at the edge of a huge area burned in the Butler II and Slide Fires in 2007. The Butler Fire was originally triggered by lightning and was thought to be under control, but a hot spot, rekindled by strong winds, jumped the fire line and scorched more than 20,000 acres including miles of the PCT. Once-tall pines now litter the slopes like charred matchsticks. Magnificent but desolate views extend west over the San Bernardino Mountains and all the way to Mt. Baldy.

Cross several seasonal creeks, and parallel Forest Road 2N81 to reach Little Bear Spring Trail Camp in 3.3 miles. Here you will find a picnic table, corral, and elaborate solar outhouse in a bleak scorched clear-cut. Water may be available at a spigot but should be treated first.

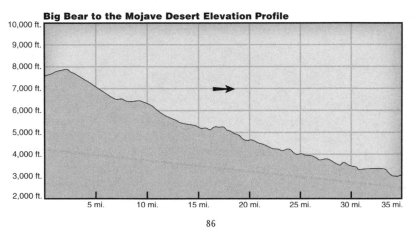

Big Bear to the Mojave Desert Elevation Profile

Upper reaches of Holcomb Creek after the Butler II fire with the Mount Baldy group looming in the distance

Most backpackers will prefer to seek camping sites along the trail in the forested areas ahead rather than stay at this depressing site.

In 0.4 mile, reach Coxey Truck Trail (3N14). Easily ford Holcomb Creek on the road bed. The PCT resumes on the north side of the willow-lined creek above Forest Road 3N93, a jeep track that is temporarily closed because of the Butler II Fire. Look for beaver dams along this portion of the creek.

After a pleasant stretch near the creek, the trail climbs onto a ridge to bypass a difficult narrow section of Holcomb Creek. Enjoy the views of Butler Peak to the south. Broad Redonda Ridge on the north marks the edge of the massive 1999 Willow Fire, which ravaged 63,000 acres north of Lake Arrowhead after being started by arson. Scrub oak is regenerating, but the pines have been wiped out. Good

Crossing Holcomb Creek

vistas and dry camping can be found along the trail. Eventually, make some short switchbacks and descend back toward the creek, paralleling above the rocky gorge for some distance. Cross the Cienega Larga tributary 5.6 miles from Coxey Truck Trail.

In another 0.7 mile, the trail descends to cross Holcomb Creek at a poorly marked ford, which may be tricky in the spring if the logs and rocks hikers use to cross are submerged or slippery. Thrash westward on the south side of the creek through a tangle of downed trees and pass Forest Road 3N16, which crosses the river here. Pleasant small campsites can be found along this segment of Holcomb Creek. The trail tends to be in poor condition because of rocks, roots, and washouts. In 0.3 mile, cross back to the north side at another poorly marked ford just before a tributary comes in from the south. After an easy 1.0 mile, pass the Cienega Redonda tributary. In another 0.6

mile, make your fourth and final ford of Holcomb Creek by wading through a deep pool.

Another 0.2 mile brings you to Holcomb Crossing Trail Camp, where you may enjoy a welcome respite on soft duff beneath the tall Jeffrey pines. This campsite is ideal for a two-day trip, with chickadees, owls, and woodpeckers to keep you company. Fill up your water bottles before you leave because the next reliable water is at the Deep Creek bridge in 4.2 miles.

Continue westward for 0.3 mile to cross the heavily rutted ATV track 1W17 descending from Crab Flats. The diverse forest along Holcomb Creek includes sugar and Coulter pines and incense cedars, as well as the Jeffrey pines, white firs, and black oaks common in the higher country. In another 0.3 mile, pass Bench Camp, another fine campsite, marking the end of your travel along Holcomb Creek. Gradually climb onto the slopes to the south, and in 0.6 mile, pass a junction with trail 2W08, which leads up the hill to Forest Road 3N34 at Tent Peg Group Camp.

The next segment of the trail was burned in the 2003 Old Fire, which was triggered by arson and consumed 91,000 acres and 993 homes. After a long slog through the blackened landscape, make a few switchbacks and reach the Deep Creek bridge in 3.0 miles. This beautiful arch has been repaired after a burning pine smashed it during the fire. Camping and access to water may be found near the bridge. On the far side of the bridge, a spur trail leads 0.1 mile south to Splinters Cabin Trailhead, an optional exit point (see Hike 17, page 93).

The PCT turns abruptly northward to follow the canyon of Deep Creek. The narrow path clings to the canyon wall, weaving to avoid crumbling granite cliffs. Enjoy the fine views of the rapids and pools more than 100 feet below. The first segment is shaded by oaks, but the trail soon recrosses the perimeter of the Willow Fire and becomes fully exposed to the sun. Butler Peak now appears far to the east, providing an indication of the distance you have covered. Deer

Mountain's chaparral-clad slopes are one of the main landmarks to the northeast.

Pass the confluence with Holcomb Creek on the south side of the mountain, then the heavily vegetated canyon of Devils Hole on the north flank. The trail soon drops to meet Forest Road 3N34D, 2.8 miles from the bridge. A short detour down this road leads to a fine pool in Deep Creek, where hearty swimmers may cool off in the frigid waters.

The next trail segment winds northwest through remote, rarely visited country. The canyon walls are initially steep and rugged but gradually give way to gentler slopes. Luna Mountain looms high above to the north. Coxey Creek enters the canyon on the far side. After 4.5 miles, reach a ford across Willow Creek.

The canyon soon turns westward again. As you approach Deep Creek Hot Springs, signs of humans become clear again. Various trails lead down to the creek, where camping is possible on the sandy banks. Stoves are permitted, but campfires are prohibited. In 1.9 miles, reach the popular hot spring, which bustles with a colorful cast of characters almost any time of year. *Camping at the hot spring is prohibited.* For obvious reasons, glass bottles are also forbidden.

After leaving the hot springs, continue west for 2.1 miles to another bridge crossing to the rugged north side of Deep Creek. In 2.8 miles, switchback down to the east end of the Mojave Forks Dam. The trail drops down to ford the creek again and follows the south bank to reach Highway 173 in 1.2 miles.

Holcomb Creek

DIRECTIONS   This trip requires a 1½-hour car shuttle between the Mojave Forks Dam and Polique Canyon Rd.

Arrange for a vehicle at the west end of this hike where the PCT crosses Highway 173 near the Mojave Forks Dam. You can reach it from Interstate 15 at Exit 131 by driving east on Highway 138 for 8.6 miles, then turning left on Highway 173 and following it 7.5 miles to the signed PCT crossing, 0.6 mile east of Arrowhead Lake Rd.

To reach the east end of the hike, drive west 0.6 mile, then turn right (north) on Arrowhead Lake Rd. In 5.7 miles, turn right (east) on Rock Springs Rd. In 2.8 miles, the road becomes Roundup Way. Continue east another 2.0 miles, then turn left (north) on Central Rd. In 3.5 miles, turn right (east) on Bear Valley Rd. In 2.7 miles, turn right on Highway 18. Proceed 10.6 miles to the junction with Highway 247. Turn right at the junction to stay on Highway 18, and continue 19.7 miles up to Big Bear City. When the highway turns left (south), continue 5.5 miles west on North Shore Dr. (Highway 38), then turn right onto Polique Canyon Rd. (Forest Road 2N09) at mile marker 038 SBD 54.04. Proceed 2.3 miles to the top of the ridge, where you will see the signed Holcomb View Trail. Limited parking is available along the side of the road just beyond.

PERMIT   Forest Adventure Pass required at Polique Canyon Rd.

OTHER POINTS OF INTEREST   Camping is available at Mojave River Forks Campground near the western trailhead. Extensive camping and lodging is available in the Big Bear area, including at Serrano Campground on Highway 38 just east of Polique Canyon Rd.

17 Upper Deep Creek

SCENERY: ✿ ✿ ✿ ✿
CHILDREN: ✿ ✿ ✿
DIFFICULTY: ✿ ✿
SOLITUDE: ✿ ✿ ✿ ✿
  DISTANCE: *6 miles (out-and-back)*
ELEVATION GAIN: *600'*

HIKING TIME: *3 hours*
BEST TIMES: *October–June*
USFS PCT MAP: Volume 2
OUTSTANDING FEATURES: *Proposed Wild and Scenic River*

Deep Creek, the largest tributary of the Mojave River, is one of the wildest parts of the San Bernardino Mountains. The PCT clings to narrow ledges on crumbling cliffs high above the water as it follows the dramatic canyon. This popular trip leads from Splinters Cabin to a swimming hole along the creek.

Deep Creek is a state designated Wild Trout Stream famous among anglers for its native rainbow and brown trout populations. Barbless hooks are required, and artificial bait is forbidden. The catch is limited to two fish, with a minimum length of 8 inches.

This trip starts at Splinters Cabin, a fishing cabin built in 1922 by Le Roy Raymond. Mr. Raymond's wife commented that everything he built was full of splinters, and hence he

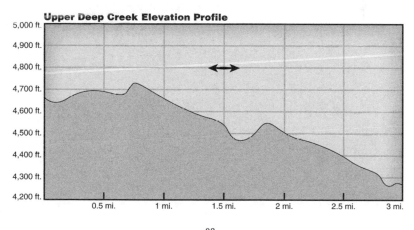

Upper Deep Creek Elevation Profile

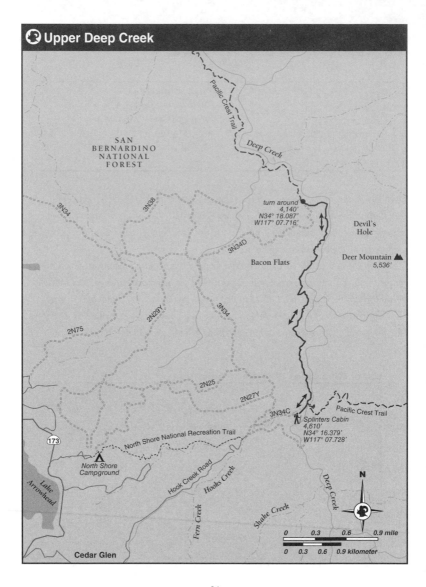

Upper Deep Creek

SAN
BERNARDINO
NATIONAL
FOREST

Pacific Crest Trail

Deep Creek

3N34

3N38

3N34D

turn around
4,140'
N34° 18.087'
W117° 07.716'

Devil's
Hole

Deer Mountain ▲
5,536'

Bacon Flats

2N29Y

3N34

2N75

2N25

2N27Y

3N34C

Splinters Cabin
4,610'
N34° 16.379'
W117° 07.728'

Pacific Crest Trail

173

North Shore National Recreation Trail

North Shore
Campground

Hook Creek Road

Hooks Creek

Fern Creek

Shake Creek

Deep Creek

Lake
Arrowhead

N

| 0 | 0.3 | 0.6 | 0.9 mile |
| 0 | 0.3 | 0.6 | 0.9 kilometer |

Cedar Glen

Happy hiker along Deep Creek

*gave the cabin its name in her honor. The walls, constructed of river rock, are still stand-
ing, shaded by a ramada.*

🥾🥾 From Splinters Cabin, look for a sign pointing south to the
PCT. Cross Little Bear Creek on rocks and logs to reach the Pacific
Crest Trail at an impressive bridge over Deep Creek in 0.1 mile.
Don't cross the bridge (unless you want to take in the view or try your luck
fishing on the far bank), but instead hike north on the west side of
the creek. The well-built trail stays high above the water to bypass the
sheer cliffs of the canyon. After threading through tenacious groves
of oaks, the trail enters a long shadeless stretch burnt in the 1999
Willow Fire. Although the trail is in good condition, a careless stum-
ble off the edge could have fatal consequences.

In 1.2 miles, pass the confluence of Holcomb Creek. The burnt
slopes of Deer Mountain rise steeply above Deep Creek on the east.

In another 1.1 miles, reach the northern edge of Deer Mountain where a heavily overgrown canyon carries the evocative name of Devil's Hole. In another 0.5 mile, round a bend to the west and descend to reach an intersection with Forest Road 3N34D from Bacon Flats. Turn right and follow the road a short way to Deep Creek. A broad swimming hole will tempt hikers to cool off in the warmer months. Note that this area gets some ATV traffic and is the only spot in the area where vehicles can ford Deep Creek (when water levels are low).

Return the way you came. Or if you would prefer a change of scenery, follow 3N34D up to Bacon Flats, then turn left and follow 3N34 back to Splinters Cabin. This variation adds a mile to the trip.

DIRECTIONS   From Highway 173 on the east shore of Lake Arrowhead, drive east on Hook Creek Rd. through the village of Cedar Glen. In 2.3 miles, pass a gate and continue on Forest Road 2N26Y. Drive 0.9 mile, then stay left at a junction with 3N34. In 0.2 mile, make a right turn on 3N34C. In 0.4 mile, park at Splinters Cabin Trailhead at the road's end. If 3N34C is gated closed, park outside, taking care not to block the gate, and start walking from the gate.

PERMIT   Forest Adventure Pass required.

OTHER POINTS OF INTEREST   Northshore Campground by Lake Arrowhead is conveniently located in this area. Hikers can access the trailhead from the campground on foot by way of North Shore National Recreation Trail; this variation adds 2.5 miles each way.

18 Deep Creek Hot Springs

SCENERY: ☆ ☆ ☆ ☆
CHILDREN: ☆ ☆
DIFFICULTY: ☆ ☆ ☆
SOLITUDE: ☆ ☆
DISTANCE: 12 miles (out-and-back)

ELEVATION GAIN: 800'
HIKING TIME: 6 hours or 1 night
BEST TIMES: September–May
USFS PCT MAP: Volume 2
OUTSTANDING FEATURES: Hot spring

Deep Creek Hot Springs is a legendary natural spring on the northern flank of the San Bernardino Mountains. The clothing-optional pools attract a colorful mixture of families, hikers, and hippies. The shortest and most popular approach is from Bowen Ranch, to the north. This alternative route, via the PCT, makes you truly earn your soaking. Although you are likely to have company at the hot springs almost any day of the year, you may find solitude on the long trail.

Camping is prohibited near the hot springs, but some sites are available about a mile farther east below the PCT. Leave your glass bottles behind. Bring plenty of water if the weather will be warm.

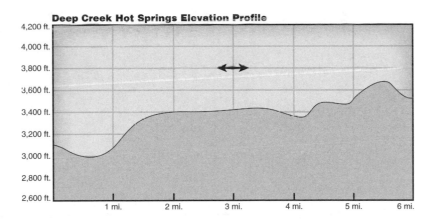

Deep Creek Hot Springs Elevation Profile

🌀 Deep Creek Hot Springs

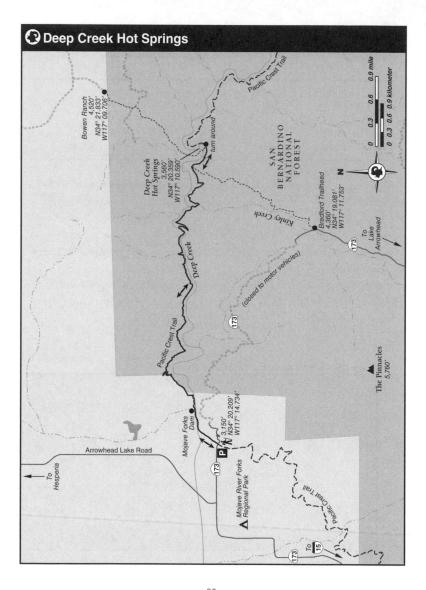

Bowen Ranch
4,520'
N34° 21.833'
W117° 09.706'

Pacific Crest Trail

turn around

Deep Creek
Hot Springs
3,560'
N34° 20.359'
W117° 10.590'

SAN
BERNARDINO
NATIONAL
FOREST

Kinley Creek

Bradford Trailhead
4,360'
N34° 19.081'
W117° 11.753'

Deep Creek

To
Lake
Arrowhead

173

Pacific Crest Trail

(closed to motor vehicles)

173

The Pinnacles
5,760'

Mojave Forks
Dam

3,150'
N34° 20.209'
W117° 14.734'

P

Arrowhead Lake Road

173

To
Hesperia

Mojave River Forks
Regional Park

Pacific Crest Trail

173 To 15

N

0   0.3   0.6   0.9 mile

0   0.3   0.6   0.9 kilometer

Deep Creek Hot Springs

🚶🚶 Follow the PCT northeast for 0.8 mile. The flats north of the trail and near the river have been severely impacted by illegal ATV use. Follow the PCT east along the south side of the Mojave Forks Dam past the dam's gates. When you can go no further, the trail abruptly turns left (north), crosses a brushy area, and fords Deep Creek. On the north side of the creek, look for a PCT sign and follow a rough path east and then up onto the spillway at the east end of the dam where the clear trail resumes. The PCT then leads east 0.4 mile up onto the Mojave Forks Dam to the spillway at the east end.

Climb steep switchbacks and then follow the PCT east as it contours above Deep Creek. In 1.8 miles, pass an unsigned fork on the right leading down to a waterfall overlook. This otherwise idyllic viewpoint is marred with extensive graffiti. Also, beware of poison oak along this part of the PCT. Be careful on the steep cliffs by the overlook.

In another 1.1 miles, cross back to the south side of Deep Creek on a graceful arched bridge. Continue east 2.0 miles to the hot springs. Return the way you came.

DIRECTIONS From Interstate 15 south of the Cajon Pass, take Exit 131 for Highway 138 and go east for 8.3 miles. Turn left onto Highway 173 and continue 7.6 miles. Park at the PCT trailhead where the highway turns to dirt.

PERMIT None. Camping is prohibited at Deep Creek Hot Springs.

OTHER POINTS OF INTEREST Camping is available nearby at Mojave River Forks Regional Park.

Lower Deep Creek

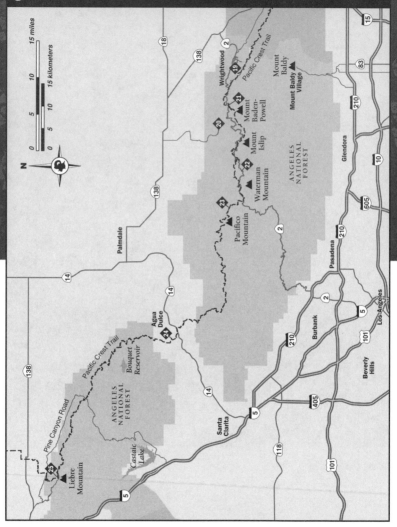

San Gabriel Mountains

4

SAN GABRIEL MOUNTAINS

19 Wrightwood to Baldy

SCENERY: ✿ ✿ ✿ ✿ ✿	HIKING TIME: *8 hours or 2 days*
CHILDREN: ✿	BEST TIMES: *June–October*
DIFFICULTY: ✿ ✿ ✿ ✿	TOM HARRISON MAP: Angeles High Country
SOLITUDE: ✿ ✿	USFS PCT MAP: Volume 2
DISTANCE: *12 miles (one-way with shuttle)*	OUTSTANDING FEATURES: *Dramatic views*
ELEVATION GAIN: *5,100'*	

Sometimes the best part of hiking the PCT is getting to and from the trail. This trip traverses Mount San Antonio from north to south. Affectionately known as Baldy, Mt. San Antonio is the crown of the San Gabriel Mountains at an elevation of 10,064 feet. While this trip involves less than a mile on the PCT, the stunning views along Baldy's North Backbone make this trip well worth the effort. Portions of the trail are very steep and loose; trekking poles may be helpful.

This one-way hike takes you from Wrightwood south over Pine Mountain, Dawson Peak, and Mt. San Antonio to Manker Flats. In reverse it has about the same elevation gain, but the southbound route has arguably better views and culminates on the summit of Baldy.

🚶🚶 Walk up Acorn Dr. to a gate in 0.5 mile. Pass the gate and continue up a dirt road to a sign on the left for the Acorn Trail in another 0.3 mile. Follow the Acorn Trail through a beautiful forest of oaks, Jeffrey pines, white firs, and incense cedar. As the trail switchbacks southward climbing toward Blue Ridge, watch for the graceful silhouettes of the long-coned sugar pines. The Acorn Trail ends atop the ridge in 2.0 miles at a signed junction with the PCT.

Turn left (west) and follow the PCT toward Wright Mtn. as it contours just above Forest Road 2N06. You may notice a use trail on the left leading to the summit of Wright Mountain, but stay on the PCT as it veers south and winds around the mountain. Enjoy the imposing views of Pine Mountain to the south. When you reach the prominent saddle between Wright Mountain and Pine Mountain in 0.9 mile, leave the PCT and pick a path down to the road.

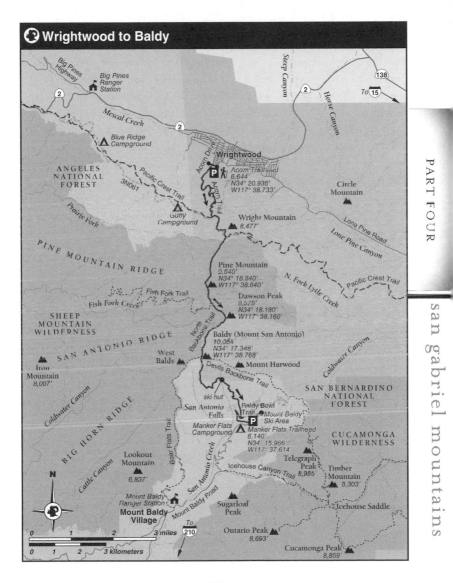

Big Pines Highway

Big Pines Ranger Station

2

Steep Canyon

138

To 15

2

Horse Canyon

Mescal Creek

2

Blue Ridge Campground

Wrightwood

ANGELES NATIONAL FOREST

Pacific Crest Trail

3N06I

Acorn Drive

Acorn Trailhead
6,644'
N34° 20.936'
W117° 38.733'

Circle Mountain

Prairie Fork

Gully Campground

Acorn Trail

Wright Mountain
8,477'

Lone Pine Road

Lone Pine Canyon

PINE MOUNTAIN RIDGE

Pine Mountain
9,640'
N34° 18.840'
W117° 38.640'

N. Fork Lytle Creek

Pacific Crest Trail

Fish Fork Trail

Fish Fork Creek

Dawson Peak
9,575'
N34° 18.180'
W117° 38.160'

SHEEP MOUNTAIN WILDERNESS

North Backbone Trail

Baldy (Mount San Antonio)
10,064'
N34° 17.348'
W117° 38.768'

SAN ANTONIO RIDGE

West Baldy

Coldwater Canyon

Iron Mountain
8,007'

Devils Backbone Trail

Mount Harwood

SAN BERNARDINO NATIONAL FOREST

Coldwater Canyon

ski hut

San Antonio Falls

Baldy Bowl Trail

Mount Baldy Ski Area

BIG HORN RIDGE

Manker Flats Campground

Manker Flats Trailhead
6,140'
N34° 15.966'
W117° 37.614'

CUCAMONGA WILDERNESS

Cattle Canyon

Bear Flats Trail

San Antonio Creek

Lookout Mountain
6,837'

Icehouse Canyon Trail

Telegraph Peak
8,985'

Timber Mountain
8,303'

N

Mount Baldy Ranger Station

Mount Baldy Village

Mount Baldy Road

Sugarloaf Peak

Icehouse Saddle

To 210

Ontario Peak
8,693'

Cucamonga Peak
8,859'

0   1   2   3 miles

0   1   2   3 kilometers

The unsigned North Backbone Trail leads south toward Pine Mtn. It briefly drops into the saddle, passing the Sheep Mountain Wilderness boundary sign. If you scan the mountainsides closely, you'll see trails left by Nelson bighorn sheep. On a lucky day, attentive hikers may even glimpse the shy animals that make their home on these forbidding slopes. Unfortunately, mountain lion predation has decimated their population, and they may soon be gone from this range.

Your trail begins a long and steep climb directly up the north ridge of Pine Mtn. The forest abruptly shifts to lodgepole pines, and the views in all directions get better and better as you climb. The summit of Pine Mtn. is about 100 feet east of the trail. When you reach the highest point of the trail in 1.4 miles, it's worth the short walk across shards of schist to reach the true summit.

The views here are some of the best of the trip, encompassing all of Southern California's highest peaks. Looking west, Mt. Baden-Powell's sheer slopes tower over the headwaters of the San Gabriel River. To the left, you can look across the San Gabriel Mountains all the way to the observatory atop Mt. Wilson. To the south are dramatic views of Dawson Peak and Mt. Baldy. To the east, towering San

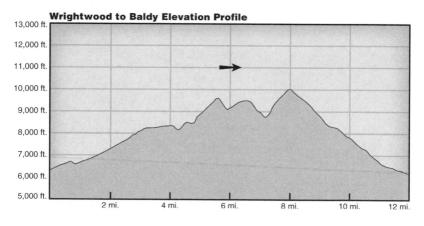

Wrightwood to Baldy Elevation Profile

Baldy's North Ridge

Gorgonio and San Jacinto guard the passage from the Los Angeles Basin to the Colorado Desert. To the north lies the vast expanse of the Mojave Desert.

Descend the south ridge to another saddle. In late summer, you may find bushes laden with tasty red wild currants alongside the trail. Soon after passing the saddle (0.4 mile from the summit), pass a sign indicating the lightly used trail on the right to Fish Fork Creek. Stay left and climb 0.5 mile to Dawson Peak. The trail remains west of the summit, but you may again wish to make a 100-yard detour to the high point. Descend 0.6 mile to yet another saddle between Dawson and Baldy before making the steep 0.7-mile final push to Baldy's breathtaking summit.

Wood grain on weather–beaten tree

No fewer than five trails converge upon Baldy's summit, so take care that you descend the right one, especially when visibility is poor. The Devils Backbone Trail leads east past Mt. Harwood to the ski area. Bear Ridge Trail leads west past a wooden post to make a long descent to Baldy Village. Just right of Bear Ridge Trail, a use trail leads to the summit of West Baldy and down the harrowing San Antonio Ridge to Iron Mountain. But this trip follows unsigned Baldy Bowl Trail, which leads due south past scraggly pines struggling for their lives on these harsh slopes.

After you drop down the ridge to the south for 0.5 mile, look for a sign confirming that you are on Baldy Bowl Trail. In the drainage below, you may see scraps of a C46 Commando that clipped the ridge and cartwheeled down the canyon on an overcast day in 1945. Follow the trail as it leads farther down the ridge and then turns east to drop down near the south edge of the Baldy Bowl in 0.5 mile. Continue across a talus field, and pass San Antonio Creek to reach the Sierra Club ski hut in 0.6 mile, where you may sometimes find water. The trail makes its final 1.7-mile descent to reach a dirt ski area service road. Turn right at this junction (easy to miss if you are coming from below), and follow the dirt road 0.9 mile down past a hairpin turn near San Antonio Falls to the terminus at Manker Flats.

Backpackers will find awesome but exposed camping atop Baldy and at many points in the first mile down the Baldy Bowl Trail. It is also possible to camp near the saddle between Pine and Dawson.

DIRECTIONS   This trip requires a 1½-hour car shuttle. If you have a large enough group, consider having half the group hike in each direction and exchange keys atop Dawson Peak.

Position one vehicle at Manker Flats. From Interstate 210, exit north on Mountain Ave. in Upland. Mountain Ave. veers right, then back left, passes San Antonio Dam and San Antonio Creek, and eventually reaches a T-junction with Mt. Baldy Rd. Turn right and drive 9 miles up to Manker Flats.

Leave one vehicle here, then drive back down to Interstate 210. Head east, then take Interstate 15 north. Just below Cajon Pass, take Exit 131 northwest on Highway 138. Go 8.8 miles, and then head west on Highway 2 for 5.4 miles into Wrightwood. Turn left on Spruce St., then right on Apple Ave. in two blocks, and then left on Acorn Dr. in another block. Follow Acorn as it winds for 0.6 mile to where it becomes a private road, and park off the pavement.

PERMIT   Forest Adventure Pass required at Manker Flats.

OTHER POINTS OF INTEREST   The Wrightwood area is full of campgrounds. Blue Ridge Campground, on Forest Road 3N06, is conveniently located near the south end of the Acorn Trail if you want to shorten the trip. The eight sites are first-come, first-served and charge no fees beyond the Adventure Pass requirement. Wrightwood is a resort town with multiple options for lodging and dining.

20 Angeles Crest Loop

SCENERY: ☆ ☆ ☆ ☆	HIKING TIME: *13 hours or 2—3 days*
CHILDREN: ☆	BEST TIMES: *June—October*
DIFFICULTY: ☆ ☆ ☆ ☆ ☆	TOM HARRISON MAP: Angeles High Country
SOLITUDE: ☆ ☆ ☆ ☆	USFS PCT MAP: Volume 2
DISTANCE: *23 miles (loop)*	OUTSTANDING FEATURES: *Grand loop through*
ELEVATION GAIN: *5,500'*	*the high country*

This strenuous and spectacular loop samples many of the pleasures of the San Gabriel Mountains. Starting in the desert on the north side of the range, the trip climbs to the summit of Mt. Baden-Powell and follows the PCT along its highest segment in the San Gabriels before returning via dramatic Big Rock Creek canyon. Along the way, you'll encounter sandstone outcrops, creeks, springs, wildflowers, breathtaking views, and many of the plant communities of the San Gabriels. Peak baggers have the option of visiting at least six summits along the crest.

If you are doing this trip as a backpacking trip, availability of water is a key concern. Lamel Springs may slow to a dubious trickle by late summer, making Little Jimmy Springs the only reliable water on the long trek between Vincent Gap and Islip Saddle. Consider stashing water in a vehicle at Vincent Gap. Always treat water before using it.

Campsites are also a factor. Little Jimmy Trail Camp is an excellent site, but is poorly situated for those planning a two-day trip. Exposed but spectacular camping is available on the summit of Mt. Baden-Powell, and many spots on the ridge between Baden-Powell and Mt. Hawkins are suitable for small groups to pitch tents. For a three-day trip, consider hiking the loop in reverse, making a first camp at Little Jimmy and a second dry camp atop Baden-Powell.

🥾 This hike begins at South Fork Campground. There is a large trailhead parking area immediately north of the campsites. Signed Manzanita Trail starts on the east side of the road opposite the parking area. Your first goal is to follow the trail east up the canyon to Vincent Gap, a gradual ascent of 2,000 feet over 5.7

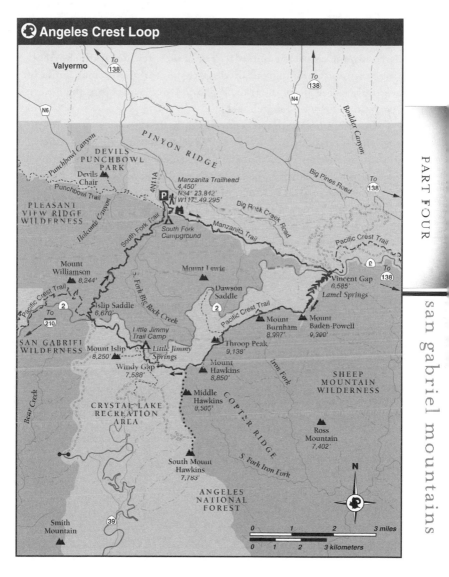

Angeles Crest Loop

Valyermo

To 138

N6

N4

To 138

PINYON RIDGE

Boulder Canyon

DEVILS PUNCHBOWL PARK

Devils Chair

Punchbowl Canyon

Punchbowl Trail

4N11A

Big Pines Road

To 138

Manzanita Trailhead
4,450'
N34° 23.813'
W117° 49.295'

PLEASANT VIEW RIDGE WILDERNESS

Holcomb Canyon

South Fork Trail

South Fork Campground

Manzanita Trail

Big Rock Creek Road

Pacific Crest Trail

Mount Williamson
8,244'

Mount Lewis

Vincent Gap
6,585'
Lamel Springs

To 138

Pacific Crest Trail

2

210

Islip Saddle
6,670'

S. Fork Big Rock Creek

Dawson Saddle

2

Pacific Crest Trail

Mount Burnham
8,997'

Mount Baden-Powell
9,399'

SAN GABRIEL WILDERNESS

Little Jimmy Trail Camp

Mount Islip
8,250'

Little Jimmy Springs

Throop Peak
9,138'

Windy Gap
7,588'

Mount Hawkins
8,850'

Bear Creek

CRYSTAL LAKE RECREATION AREA

Middle Hawkins
8,505'

COPTER RIDGE

Iron Fork

SHEEP MOUNTAIN WILDERNESS

Ross Mountain
7,402'

South Mount Hawkins
7,783'

S. Fork Iron Fork

ANGELES NATIONAL FOREST

39

N

Smith Mountain

0   1   2   3 miles

0   1   2   3 kilometers

miles. The trail leads through yuccas, scrub oak, and other chaparral climbing above the east side of the campground as it ascends toward a prominent sandstone outcrop. You'll see a few use trails shortcutting down to the campground. Despite the trail name, manzanita is relatively scarce along the trail. Bigcone Douglas firs join the desert vegetation at the first switchback.

In 0.8 mile, an unmarked trail on the left leads to a vista point atop the outcrop; this short detour is recommended. At the time of this writing, portions of the trail have been washed out or damaged by small avalanches, but it is still readily passable. In another 1.1 miles, look for a trail to the left leading down to the small settlement of Big Rock. Cross a number of seasonal creeks and the main fork of Big Rock Creek descending Dorr Canyon. Some stretches of the trail are pleasantly shaded beneath groves of oaks. Around 6,000 feet, the desert vegetation gives way to a forest of sugar and Jeffrey pines and white firs before reaching Vincent Gap.

Cross the Angeles Crest Highway to the large parking lot on the south side. Be sure to take the PCT, which switchbacks southward up Mt. Baden-Powell, not one of the other trails radiating from the

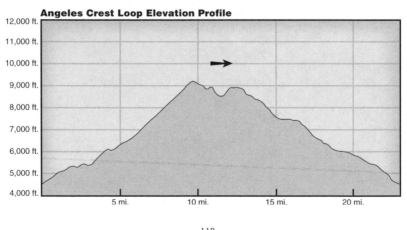

Angeles Crest Loop Elevation Profile

Little Jimmy Springs

gap. The next stretch of trail is described in detail in Hike 21 (page 116). In brief, climb 3.9 miles to Mt. Baden-Powell, passing Lamel Springs en route. Follow the PCT 2.4 miles to a trail junction below Throop Peak, passing Mt. Burnham along the way. Peak baggers might wish to stay on the ridge and climb Mt. Burnham rather than staying on the PCT, which contours around the north side.

At a junction by Throop Peak, the right fork descends to Dawson Saddle, but this trip stays left on the PCT. Watch for a second unmarked fork on the right in 100 feet leading 0.3 mile to Throop Peak, but continue on the PCT around the south side of Throop.

This high ridge between Baden-Powell and Windy Gap is a favorite stretch of the PCT in the San Gabriel Mountains. Keep your eyes out for gliders, whose skilled pilots hug the ridges in search of lift. In 0.9 mile, the trail crosses back to the north side of the ridge. Another unsigned trail on the left leads 0.2 mile to Mt. Hawkins, named for Nellie Hawkins, a popular waitress who charmed visitors at nearby Squirrel Inn in the first decade of the twentieth century.

Continue west on the PCT. Many of the trees in this area were wiped out by the 2002 Curve Fire, tragically triggered by a ritual involving animal sacrifice and candles gone out of control. You may notice a sign for Lily Spring, half a mile below the PCT, but the trail to the spring was obliterated in the fire. In 0.6 mile, reach a junction with the Hawkins Ridge Trail that leads 0.5 mile south to Middle Hawkins Peak and onward to South Hawkins.

Continue west 1.4 miles to aptly named Windy Gap, where trails veer off toward Crystal Lake and Mt. Islip. Islip's summit, 1.0 mile from the PCT, offers excellent views. The peak was named for George Islip, a mountain man who settled in the area in the second half of the nineteenth century.

In another 0.2 mile, the PCT passes a turnoff on the right for Little Jimmy Springs. Even if you don't need the water, it's worth the short detour to enjoy a break on the log benches beside the spring beneath a magnificent incense cedar. The path continues past the spring to rejoin the PCT nearby. In yet another 0.2 mile, reach pleasant Little Jimmy Trail Camp, the best campsite along this hike. Contour along the north slopes of Mt. Islip above Angeles Crest Highway for 2.1 miles before descending to Islip Saddle.

Two poorly marked trails depart from the northwest corner of the parking lot at Islip Saddle. The PCT begins climbing toward Mt. Williamson, but we take South Fork Trail to the right that descends into the wild V-shaped canyon cut by the South Fork of Big Rock Creek. You are now entering Pleasant View Ridge Wilderness, established by Congress in 2009. The well-built trail follows a steady grade, periodically weaving in and out of side canyons. Once a key route for foot and mule traffic into the high country, it has fallen into disuse now that the Angeles Crest Highway provides easy vehicle access. In places, it has been damaged by incessant rockfall. In others, it clings tenuously to steep cliffs.

In 5.1 miles, the trail makes two final switchbacks and drops down to the creek. The trail is presently washed out in this area and difficult to follow. Cross the creek and walk north along the east bank. Soon you will see South Fork Campground on the right. Follow the trail between the creek and campground for 0.3 mile to reach the trailhead parking where this grand loop began.

DIRECTIONS From Highway 138 between Palmdale and Victorville, turn south on 165th St. This junction is 26.5 miles northwest on Hwy. 138 from Interstate 15, or 16.7 miles east on Hwy. 138 from Highway 14. In 1.9 miles, the road veers left and becomes Bob's Gap Road, which leads southeast, then west, then south again. When it ends in 4.5 miles at Highway N6 (Big Pines Rd.), turn left and go southeast for 0.3 mile, then turn right onto Big Rock Creek Rd. Proceed 2.4 miles to a turnoff for South Fork Campground on the right. Follow this graded dirt Forest Road 4N11A 0.9 mile to the campground.

PERMIT Forest Adventure Pass required.

OTHER POINTS OF INTEREST South Fork Campground is a convenient place to stay the night before the trip. The first-come, first-served campground has a primitive ambience and offers no tap water but is free and located close to the creek (treat the water before drinking it).

21 Mount Baden-Powell

SCENERY: ✿ ✿ ✿ ✿	HIKING TIME: *5 hours*
CHILDREN: ✿ ✿	BEST TIMES: *June–October*
DIFFICULTY: ✿ ✿ ✿	TOM HARRISON MAP: Angeles High Country
SOLITUDE: ✿ ✿	USFS PCT MAP: Volume 2
DISTANCE: *8 miles (one-way with shuttle)*	OUTSTANDING FEATURES: *High ridge and*
ELEVATION GAIN: *3,700'*	*sweeping views*

Mount Baden-Powell, at 9,399 feet, is the second tallest mountain in the San Gabriel range after Baldy and its subsidiary summits. The mountain is named for the British Army officer who founded the Boy Scouts. While you are unlikely to find solitude on this popular peak, it's hard not to enjoy the panoramic views and majestic limber pines.

This hike begins at Vincent Gap. Some hikers return the same way. However, with a bicycle or car shuttle arranged at Dawson Saddle, you can make a terrific one-way hike. Dawson Saddle is 1,300 feet higher than Vincent Gap and the ride back is an exhilarating downhill coast. If you are driving, you can make the trip less strenuous by starting at Dawson Saddle and hiking in reverse.

🥾 Several trails venture forth from the large parking area at Vincent Gap. Be sure you take the well-signed PCT from the southwest corner of the lot. A sign warns you about the dangers of ice in winter months; crampons and an ice axe are necessary well into spring in most years.

Your workout begins right away as you undertake the 40 switchbacks that lead up the mountain's great north ridge through a fine conifer forest of Jeffrey and sugar pines, white firs, and incense cedars. In 1.7 miles, watch for a sign indicating Lamel Springs to the left. The spring, graced with scarlet monkeyflower and partially protected by a wire mesh, slows to a mere trickle by the end of the summer. You're better off carrying enough of your own water for the day.

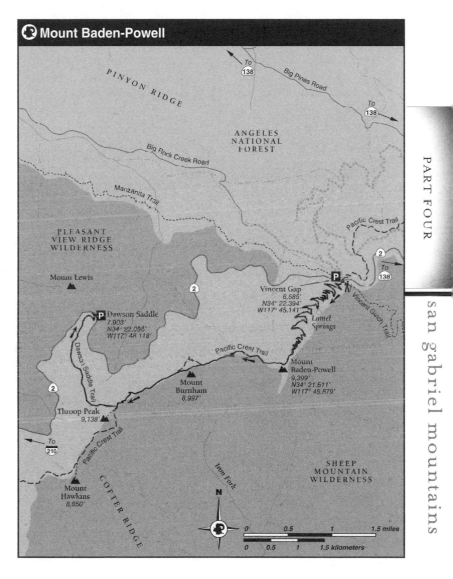

Mount Baden-Powell

PART FOUR

san gabriel mountains

To 138

Big Pines Road

To 138

PINYON RIDGE

ANGELES
NATIONAL
FOREST

Big Rock Creek Road

Manzanita Trail

Pacific Crest Trail

2
To 138

PLEASANT
VIEW RIDGE
WILDERNESS

Mount Lewis

2

Vincent Gap
6,585'
N34° 22.394'
W117° 45.141'

Vincent Gulch Trail

Dawson Saddle
7,903'
N34° 22.096'
W117° 48.118'

Lamel
Springs

Dawson Saddle Trail

Pacific Crest Trail

2

Mount
Baden-Powell
9,399'
N34° 21.511'
W117° 45.879'

Mount
Burnham
8,997'

To 210

Throop Peak
9,138'

Pacific Crest Trail

Mount
Hawkins
8,850'

COPTER RIDGE

Iron Fork

N

SHEEP
MOUNTAIN
WILDERNESS

| 0 | 0.5 | 1 | 1.5 miles |

| 0 | 0.5 | 1 | 1.5 kilometers |

At an elevation of about 8,000 feet, the forest abruptly transitions to lodgepole pines. After chugging up the switchbacks for another 2.2 miles from the spring, reach a trail junction immediately below the summit. A sign marks the Wally Waldron Tree, a gnarled and twisted limber pine believed to have been clinging tenaciously to the ridge through gales, blizzards, and droughts for approximately 1,500 years.

Take the left fork for 0.1 mile to reach the summit of Mount Baden-Powell. A monument gives tribute to Lord Baden-Powell and his contributions to scouting. Enjoy the tremendous views, including Mt. Baldy to the east, Edwards Air Force Base to the north (where the space shuttle used to land on Rogers Dry Lake), and the high ridge of the San Gabriels to the west. You are now on the edge of rugged Sheep Mountain Wilderness, which extends east to Mt. Baldy and south to the San Gabriel River.

If you don't have a shuttle, retrace your steps to Vincent Gap. Otherwise, return to the fork and head west on the PCT. Drop to a saddle, and skirt the north side of an unnamed bump on the ridge. Look for red wild currants along the ridge. In 1.1 miles, come to an

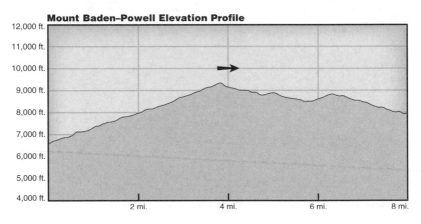

Mount Baden–Powell Elevation Profile

Wally Waldron tree, a 1,500-year-old limber pine named in honor of a Scout leader

unmarked trail junction at the next saddle just east of Mt. Burnham, a peak named for the British army officer, explorer, and Scout leader Major Frederick R. Burnham. Peak baggers will want to take the left branch over the summit, which in 0.4 mile rejoins the PCT that contoured around the north side.

Mt. Baden-Powell from near Pine Mountain

The PCT descends westward to another saddle and gradually climbs toward Throop Peak. In 0.9 mile, reach a trail junction at a broken sign. The PCT goes left, while Dawson Saddle Trail goes right. Unless you are planning to climb Throop Peak, turn right and descend the ridge 1.8 miles to Dawson Saddle, emerging at a signed trailhead 100 yards east of the saddle parking area.

Peak baggers will enjoy another short excursion to Throop Peak, named for Amos Throop, the founder of Throop University in Pasadena. The university eventually became the California Institute of Technology. Instead of descending to Dawson Saddle, go left on the PCT. In about 100 feet, look for an unsigned junction where a steep climber's trail departs the PCT to the right and ascends the ridge 0.3 mile to Throop Peak. Return to Dawson Saddle Trail after you have savored the view.

DIRECTIONS   This trip requires a 5-mile car or bicycle shuttle if you want to do it as a one-way hike rather than an out-and-back.

From Interstate 15 a few miles south of the Cajon Pass, take Exit 131 northwest on Highway 138. Follow Hwy. 138 for 8.8 miles, and then turn left on the Angeles Crest Highway (Highway 2). Drive about 20 miles to the end point just east of Dawson Saddle at mile marker 2 LA 69.6, where you will leave a bicycle or car on the north side of the road. Then drive back 5 miles back to the large parking area at Vincent Gap by mile marker 74.75 Alternatively, Highway 2 can be reached from La Cañada.

PERMIT   Forest Adventure Pass required.

OTHER POINTS OF INTEREST   For many Boy Scouts, the 53-mile Silver Moccasin Trail is a memorable rite of passage. The trail begins in Chantry Flats and ends at Vincent Gap, coinciding with the Pacific Crest Trail from Three Points eastward and with this hike for the last segment.

Numerous campgrounds can be found in the Wrightwood area.

22 Cooper Canyon Falls

SCENERY: ✿ ✿ ✿ ✿	ELEVATION GAIN: *1,300' or 800'*
CHILDREN: ✿ ✿ ✿ ✿ ✿	HIKING TIME: *3 hours*
DIFFICULTY: ✿ ✿	BEST TIMES: *April–June, September–November*
SOLITUDE: ✿ ✿ ✿	TOM HARRISON MAP: Angeles High Country
DISTANCE: *6 miles (out-and-back) or*	USFS PCT MAP: Volume 2
5 miles (one-way with shuttle)	OUTSTANDING FEATURES: *Waterfalls*

Cooper Canyon Falls is a lovely waterfall along the PCT in one of the most beautiful sections of the San Gabriel Mountains. The trip offers fine views near and far, including the wildflower-lined Cooper Creek, the healthy conifer-and-oak forest, the rugged mountains, and the tan desert far below. Wildflowers grow along the creek. If you can arrange for a shuttle, your best option is to exit via Burkhart Trail, which passes another waterfall. The best time to visit is late spring, when the waterfalls are at their most dramatic. The trail can be hot in summer. Fall offers more seclusion. With an overnight stop at Cooper Canyon Trail Camp and plenty of opportunities to play in water, this trip makes a great introductory backpacking adventure for kids.

You have two route options for this hike. Either simply hike to the falls along the PCT and then return the way you came, making a 6-mile round-trip, or exit by way of Burkhart Trail from Cooper Canyon Falls up to Buckhorn Campground, where you can meet a car or bicycle you've left there or simply hoof it back 2 miles through the campground and along the shoulder of the highway. This second option is recommended because it visits another waterfall and offers a change of scenery. Hikers and cyclists should be aware that the trip from Buckhorn back to the trailhead adds 600 feet of elevation gain.

🥾 From Cloudburst Summit, your first goal is to hike down to Cooper Canyon Trail Camp. The PCT is hidden behind the berm and is easy to overlook. Look for the PCT trail marker to the right of the yellow gate across the dirt service road. Hike northeast down the PCT as it switchbacks through an open forest of Jeffrey and sugar pines, incense cedars, white firs, and black oaks.

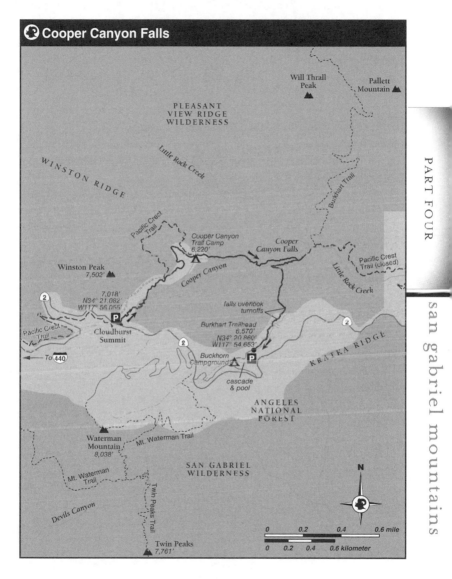

Cooper Canyon Falls

PLEASANT
VIEW RIDGE
WILDERNESS

Will Thrall
Peak

Pallett
Mountain

Little Rock Creek

WINSTON RIDGE

Burkhart Trail

Pacific Crest Trail

Cooper Canyon
Trail Camp
6,220'

Cooper
Canyon Falls

Winston Peak
7,502'

Cooper Canyon

Little Rock Creek

Pacific Crest
Trail (closed)

7,018'
N34° 21.082'
W117° 56.055'

falls overlook
turnoffs

2

Pacific Crest
Trail

Cloudburst
Summit

Burkhart Trailhead
6,570'
N34° 20.860'
W117° 54.653'

2

To 440

2

Buckhorn
Campground

KRATKA RIDGE

cascade
& pool

ANGELES
NATIONAL
FOREST

Waterman
Mountain
8,038'

Mt. Waterman Trail

N

Mt. Waterman
Trail

SAN GABRIEL
WILDERNESS

Twin Peaks Trail

Devils Canyon

| 0 | 0.2 | 0.4 | 0.6 mile |

| 0 | 0.2 | 0.4 | 0.6 kilometer |

Twin Peaks
7,761'

In 1.0 mile, the PCT crosses the service road again. From here, you may either take the PCT or the service road down to Cooper Canyon Trail Camp. The PCT makes a scenic but gratuitously long 1.6-mile meander along the rim of a side canyon, while the service road is only 0.8 mile.

Cooper Canyon Trail Camp has a handicapped-accessible outhouse and spacious first-come, first-served campsites but no tap water. It offers pleasant camping if it is not too crowded. Early in the summer, you can get water from the creek (treat before drinking), but by late summer, the camp is dry.

Follow the PCT east from the camp along the north side of Cooper Creek into Pleasant View Ridge Wilderness. In 1.3 miles, the trail crosses the creek and comes to a signed junction with Burkhart Trail (10W02). Turn left to stay on the PCT, and continue 0.1 mile to the top of Cooper Canyon Falls. Shortly beyond, look for a use trail descending to the pool at the base of the 25-foot falls. The bottom of the trail is steep and slippery and may have a rope to serve as a handline. Inspect it before trusting it.

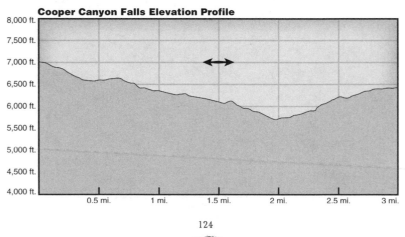

Cooper Canyon Falls Elevation Profile

Snack break at Cooper Canyon Falls

After you have enjoyed the falls, return to the junction you just passed. If you are making a one-way trip, follow the Burkhart Trail as it makes one switchback and then climbs steadily up the canyon. The sugar pines along this stretch are especially attractive, with their long cones silhouetted against the sky. Look for two use trails on the left that lead down to waterfalls along the creek. The first visits the top of a 30-foot fall; the view is not particularly good and the crumbling rock is dangerous. The second takes you to a pool at the base of a delightful 10-foot fall and is well worth the detour.

In 1.5 miles from the PCT, reach the trailhead at the outskirts of Buckhorn Campground. Note that if you continue 0.1 mile up the campground road, you pass another delightful section of the creek, with a pleasant rock for a snack break above a short cascade and cool pool. A huge overhanging rock on the far (south) side of the creek makes a good landmark for this spot.

DIRECTIONS From Interstate 210 in La Cañada Flintridge, take the Angeles Crest Highway (Highway 2) north and east 32 miles to Cloudburst Summit at mile marker 2 LA 57.21. Alternatively, the Angeles Crest Highway can be accessed from the east by way of Wrightwood. Park in a large unmarked turnout on the north side of the road, where a gate blocks access to a campground service road. A small PCT sign indicates the start of the trail. *Beware:* There are many other turnouts with dirt roads in this area.

If you wish to do a one-way hike with a shuttle, position a bicycle or second vehicle at Burkhart Trailhead. To reach the trailhead, go 1.1 miles east on Angeles Crest Highway to a turnoff for Buckhorn Campground at mile marker 2 LA 58.25. Drive through the campground and follow signs to the Burkhart Trailhead parking area. Buckhorn Campground is a beautiful place to stay.

PERMIT Forest Adventure Pass required.

OTHER POINTS OF INTEREST It was once popular to continue 4 miles along the PCT past Cooper Canyon Falls up to Eagles Roost picnic area on the Angeles Crest Highway. This portion of the PCT has been temporarily closed to protect the endangered mountain yellow-legged frog. If the trail reopens, this section is worth visiting.

23 Pacifico Mountain

SCENERY: ✿ ✿ ✿	HIKING TIME: 5 hours or 1 night
CHILDREN: ✿ ✿ ✿	BEST TIMES: April–June, September–November
DIFFICULTY: ✿ ✿ ✿	USFS PCT MAP: Volume 2
SOLITUDE: ✿ ✿ ✿ ✿	OUTSTANDING FEATURES: Views and
DISTANCE: 10 miles (out-and-back)	wildflowers
ELEVATION GAIN: 1,700'	

Pacifico Mountain (7,124 feet) is the most prominent mountain in the northwestern San Gabriel Mountains. Pacifico is Spanish for "peaceful," and you are likely to enjoy a peaceful time on this lightly visited but attractive summit. Portions of this area burned in the 2009 Station Fire, leaving a crazy quilt of new growth and pristine forest. Spring wildflowers have been exceptional in the fire's aftermath. Backpackers can camp at a small campground on the boulder-studded summit, a favorite spot for watching the sunrise (but bring your own water). When the road to the summit is open, youth groups may prefer to make this a one-way hike with their gear shuttled to the campground.

The PCT begins 150 yards back (west) along the road from the parking area. Follow it west-northwest as it winds above a drainage. The rather unimpressive, partially burned hill on the skyline to the west is Pacifico Mountain. The PCT gradually climbs through scrub oak, mountain mahogany, flannel bush (similar in size to scrub oak, but it lights up the trail with vivid yellow flowers in the spring), and the occasional Coulter pine.

The trail enters an area that burned in the 2009 Station Fire, triggered by arson. The fire consumed 160,000 acres, killed two firefighters, severely damaged the Angeles Crest Highway, and closed the forest for nearly two years. Although the tall pines will take decades to recover, the smaller vegetation is returning rapidly, accompanied by a tremendous display of wildflowers. In June 2011, I saw lupine, golden yarrow, bird's eyes, baby blue eyes, fiddlenecks, and Indian paintbrush, to name just a few.

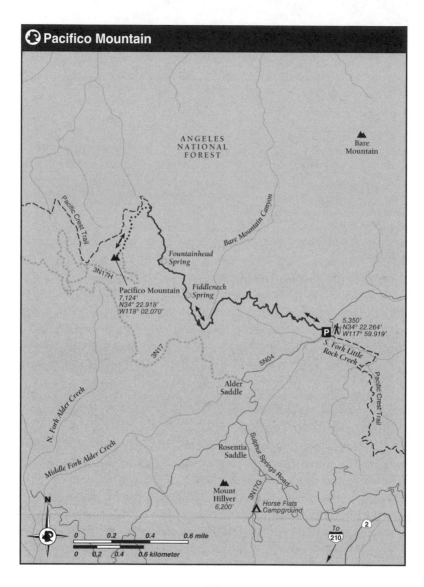

ANGELES
NATIONAL
FOREST

Bare
Mountain

Pacific Crest Trail

Bare Mountain Canyon

Fountainhead
Spring

3N17H

Pacifico Mountain
7,124'
N34° 22.918'
W118° 02.070'

Fiddleneck
Spring

5,350'
N34° 22.264'
W117° 59.919'

S. Fork Little
Rock Creek

3N17

5N04

Pacific Crest Trail

Alder
Saddle

N. Fork Alder Creek

Rosentia
Saddle

Middle Fork Alder Creek

Sulphur Springs Road

Mount
Hillyer
6,200'

3N17G

Horse Flats
Campground

To
210

2

N

0   0.2   0.4   0.6 mile
0   0.2   0.4   0.6 kilometer

Beware of standing dead trees, especially on a windy day, and never stop beneath them lest they topple on you. Moreover, the area is now infested with poodle dog bush, a rather attractive leafy green shrub displaying showy blue or purple flowers from June through August. Touching poodle dog bush causes a nasty delayed rash, including itching and blisters for unfortunate victims. The bush sprouts after the ground has been cleared by fire. It may persist for five to ten years after the fire; then its seeds remain dormant in the soil until the next fire. Exercise caution because poodle dog bush may intrude onto the trail in places.

Poodle dog bush

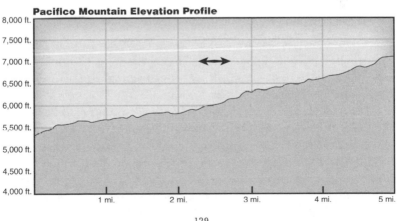

Pacifico Mountain Elevation Profile

Burnt log and wildflowers

The trail rounds a bend onto the west side of a ridge, where it is shaded by black oaks that escaped the inferno, and then reaches a prominent saddle 2.5 miles from the start. In another 0.5 mile, pass Fiddleneck Spring, surrounded by ferns and shaded beneath an incense cedar. The spring usually slows to a trickle by May. In another 0.6 mile, pass Fountainhead Spring, which may have a more robust flow but is still undependable after springtime. Continue 0.7 mile across slopes rich with wildflowers to a flat on the pine-covered north-northeast ridge of Pacifico Mountain.

Here you depart the PCT and make a cross-country ascent to the summit. Pick a path to weave among the granite boulders on the ridge. Your climb ends abruptly in 0.6 mile at Pacifico Mountain Campground, with eight pleasantly shaded sites on the mountaintop. The upper reaches of the mountain are burned in places but are mostly still clad in a healthy conifer forest of Jeffrey and sugar pines, white firs, and incense cedars. Enjoy the tremendous views to the east over Waterman, Williamson, and Mount Baden-Powell to Mt. Baldy on the distant horizon. The true high point is a 20-foot boulder with a short steel pipe oddly cemented to the apex. The climbing is tricky, and a fall would have nasty consequences; rock climbers would call it a fourth-class climb. Most hikers will be satisfied by taking a snack break at the base.

If you would prefer to make a loop, you can hike back down the dirt campground access road. This variation adds a mile but is fast, easy walking. In 1.6 miles, turn left at a junction with wide graded Forest Road 3N17. After winding above the head of Alder Creek for 3.2 miles, reach Alder Saddle and take 5N04 the last mile back to your vehicle.

DIRECTIONS From Interstate 210 in La Cañada Flintridge, take the Angeles Crest Highway (Highway 2) north and east 28.2 miles to Sulphur Springs Rd. on your left at mile marker 2 LA 52.85. This junction is also called Three Points. Alternatively, the Angeles Crest Highway can be accessed from the east by way of Wrightwood. In either case, take Sulphur Springs Rd. 3.9 miles to a fork at Alder Saddle. Turn right on paved one-lane Forest Road 5N04. In another 1.0 mile, park at a clearing on the right, immediately beyond the turnoff for Sulphur Springs Campground.

If the gate at Alder Saddle is open, it is possible for high-clearance vehicles to drive to the top of Pacifico Mountain. From Alder Saddle, turn left on graded dirt Forest Road 3N17. In 3.2 miles, turn right onto 3N17H (high-clearance vehicles recommended). Continue 1.6 miles up to the campground on the summit.

PERMIT Forest Adventure Pass required.

OTHER POINTS OF INTEREST Nearby campgrounds include Sulphur Springs, Horse Flats, and Chilao. Potable water is available at Chilao.

24 Vasquez Rocks

SCENERY: ☆ ☆ ☆ ☆	HIKING TIME: *2 hours*
CHILDREN: ☆ ☆ ☆ ☆	BEST TIMES: *October–April (8 a.m.–sunset)*
DIFFICULTY: ☆	USFS PCT MAP: Volume 2
SOLITUDE: ☆	OUTSTANDING FEATURES: *Tilted sandstone*
DISTANCE: *4 miles (loop)*	*outcrops*
ELEVATION GAIN: *300'*	

Vasquez Rocks Natural Area Park is famed for its dramatically tilted sandstone outcrops. Roughly 10 million years ago, deep layers of sediments accumulated in this region. More recently, an offshoot of the San Andreas Fault has shoved the sandstone and fanglomerate (conglomerate rocks piled up in an alluvial fan) upward to produce oddly tilted slabs. In the 1870s, the canyons and cliffs were the hideout of notorious bandit Tiburcio Vasquez and his gang, making this perhaps the only park in the state named for an outlaw.

More recently, the iconic rocks have been the backdrop to countless westerns, science fiction films, and television series. Los Angeles County acquired the 900-acre park in the 1970s. It draws large numbers of hikers, equestrians, youth groups, and picnickers who enjoy roaming among the rocks. The scramble to the top of the highest rocks is easier than it looks, and you are rewarded by breathtaking views.

The Pacific Crest Trail threads its way through the park. A great way to see the rocks up close is to make a loop out on the PCT and back along Foot Trail. A portion of the PCT is presently being rerouted to avoid following a dirt road near houses. Moreover, trails other than the PCT are poorly signed and difficult to follow in places. A maze of social trails formed by visitors hiking off the designated paths only makes the situation worse. Perhaps the situation will improve by the time you visit. In any event, it is a pleasure to wander the trails, and you are bound to find your way back to the trailhead as long as you keep alert and watch for landmarks.

🚶🚶 This trip description assumes the PCT reroute has been completed according to plan. If it is still in progress, you may find yourself following ribbons taped to bushes rather than trail markers in some stretches. The beginning of the trip may eventually be

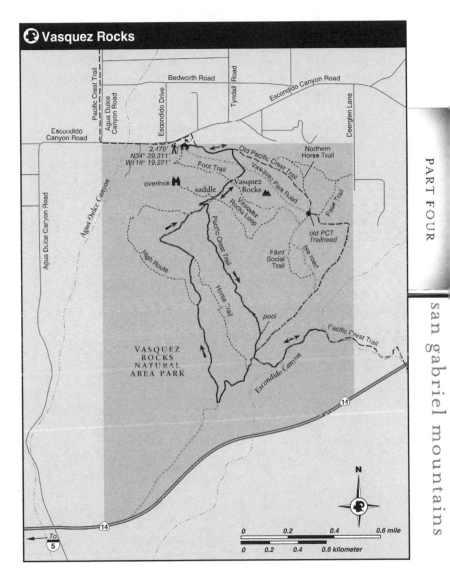

Vasquez Rocks

Bedworth Road

Pacific Crest Trail

Agua Dulce Canyon Road

Escondido Drive

Tyndall Road

Escondido Canyon Road

Deerglen Lane

Escondido Canyon Road

Northern Horse Trail

2,470'
N34° 29.311'
W118° 19.221'

Old Pacific Crest Trail

Foot Trail

Vasquez Park Road

Faint Trail

overlook

saddle

Vasquez Rocks

Vasquez Rocks Loop

Agua Dulce Canyon

old PCT Trailhead

High Route

Pacific Crest Trail

Faint Social Trail

tire road

Horse Trail

pool

VASQUEZ ROCKS NATURAL AREA PARK

Escondido Canyon

Pacific Crest Trail

14

Agua Dulce Canyon Road

N

To 5

14

| 0 | 0.2 | 0.4 | 0.6 mile |

| 0 | 0.2 | 0.4 | 0.6 kilometer |

marked better. Starting by the ranger station, hike northeast on a geology trail for 200 feet to reach the PCT. Turn right and go east for 0.1 mile. At the first intersection, turn right again, cross the road, and go southwest for 0.2 mile to reach a saddle west of the tall rocks. A new stretch of the PCT begins here. Note the landmarks here to help you find this saddle on the way back.

Follow the PCT south through a delightful canyon behind the Vasquez Rocks. In 0.8 mile, pass a seasonal pool in a creek bed and rejoin the original route of the PCT, which used to arrive at this point by descending a ridge to the left. Hike into dramatic Escondido Canyon with overhanging cliffs of sedimentary rock. Follow the seasonal creek past cottonwoods and willows through this canyon for 0.5 mile. When the canyon forks and the scenery becomes less interesting, you've reached a good point to turn around.

Return to the junction with the original PCT and turn right (south) toward Horse and Foot Trails. These trails run atop sandstone cliffs where you could imagine Vasquez and his gang preparing to ambush a posse. Foot Trail is the higher of the two, with better views and a more well-defined path, so it is recommended.

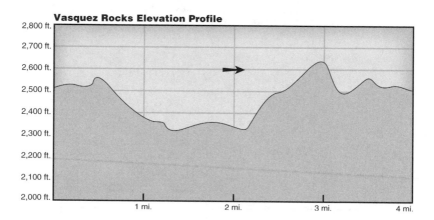

Vasquez Rocks

Follow the deteriorating fire road past the sign for Horse Trail, then up to where you can turn right onto Foot Trail, 0.3 mile from the PCT junction.

Foot Trail leads above a band of cliffs. At a fork in 0.5 mile, take the right branch labeled "54." Descend onto a broad ledge between two bands of cliffs, where you'll enjoy close-up views of the sandstone and fanglomerate. In 0.2 mile, continue straight at an unsigned junction with Horse Trail atop a hill. The next section is particularly confusing and poorly marked, with a maze of social trails branching out. Attempt to stay on the best-defined trail as it descends, turns right, and rejoins the PCT at the saddle you passed earlier. Take the PCT back to your vehicle.

san gabriel mountains

DIRECTIONS   From Highway 14, take Exit 15 north on Agua Dulce Canyon Rd. In 1.6 miles, the road turns right. In another 0.2 mile, continue straight at a stop sign onto Escondido Canyon Rd. In 0.4 mile, turn right into the Vasquez Rocks Natural Area. Park in a small lot near the ranger station just after entering the park. If there are not enough spots, more can be found a short distance farther down the park road.

PERMIT   None

OTHER POINTS OF INTEREST   From October through June, the park offers ranger-led activities from 11 a.m. to 12 p.m. on Sundays (weather permitting). The first Sunday of each month features a birds of prey presentation, while the second, third, and fourth Sundays the park offers short ranger-guided hikes. Organized groups such as the Boy Scouts may make arrangements to camp at the park.

25 Liebre Mountain

SCENERY: ✿ ✿ ✿
CHILDREN: ✿
DIFFICULTY: ✿ ✿ ✿
SOLITUDE: ✿ ✿ ✿ ✿
DISTANCE: 7 miles (out-and-back) or
9 miles (one-way with shuttle)

ELEVATION GAIN: 2,000'
HIKING TIME: 4 or 5 hours
BEST TIMES: October–June
USFS PCT MAP: Volume 2
OUTSTANDING FEATURES: Sweeping views,
wildflowers, and oak-studded ridges

Liebre Mountain is named for Rancho La Liebre ("Rabbit Ranch"), an 1846 Mexican land grant in the area. The mountain is the most prominent summit in the Liebre Range, a wedge of chaparral-clad peaks sandwiched between Interstate 5, Highway 14, and the San Andreas Fault at the edge of Antelope Valley. The range itself, geologically speaking, forms the extreme northwestern extension of the San Gabriel Mountains. This trip climbs the Pacific Crest Trail to the mountain's long oak-studded summit ridge. It offers fine views of Antelope Valley and the surrounding mountain ranges. In a wet year, the wild-flowers on the mountain are splendid.

You have two route options for this hike. One is to simply climb Liebre Mountain and return the way you came on the PCT, making a 7-mile round-trip. The other is to follow the original route of the PCT west from the summit along the ridge before dropping down to Old Ridge Road, bringing the distance up to 9 miles. The second option requires a 5-mile car or bicycle shuttle back to the starting point. The more interesting one-way trip is recommended if you have transportation and a good sense of direction.

The trailhead marks the end of the PCT's trek through the San Gabriel Mountains. Northbound thru-hikers departing this point presently face the grim prospects of a two-day march across the flat desert, largely following the California Aqueduct, to avoid private property. This is not how the PCT was originally envisioned; the route was supposed to stay high along the crest of the Tehachapi Mountains. Vast swaths of the southern Tehachapis are, however, owned by Tejon Ranch. Unfortunately, at the time the PCT was being constructed, the ranch was unwilling to negotiate a right-of-way for the trail along the crest. In 2008, Tejon Ranch reached an agreement with several conservation organizations to permanently

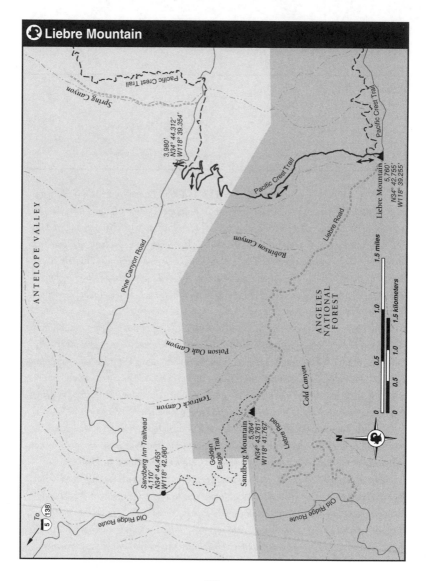

Liebre Mountain

Pacific Crest Trail

Spring Canyon

Pacific Crest Trail

3,980'
N34° 44.312'
W118° 39.354'

Pacific Crest Trail

Pacific Crest Trail

Liebre Mountain
5,760'
N34° 42.755'
W118° 39.255'

ANTELOPE VALLEY

Pine Canyon Road

Robinson Canyon

Liebre Road

Poison Oak Canyon

Tentrock Canyon

ANGELES
NATIONAL
FOREST

Cold Canyon

Sandberg Inn Trailhead
4,110'
N34° 44.453'
W118° 42.580'

Golden
Eagle Trail

Sandberg Mountain
5,364'
N34° 43.761'
W118° 41.767'

Liebre Road

Old Ridge Route

Old Ridge Route

To
5 138

N

1.5 miles

0   0.5   1.0   1.5 kilometers

0   0.5   1.0   1.5 kilometers

preserve 90 percent of the ranchland and grant a right-of-way for the PCT in exchange for the conservation organizations ending opposition to development on the remainder of the ranch. This deal will eventually lead to a PCT reroute in this area.

🚶🚶 From the trailhead, choose the PCT branch on the right that switchbacks upward. This portion of Liebre Mountain burned in the 2004 Pine Fire, which was started by arson. The chaparral has largely recovered, but the oaks and pines that once graced these slopes will take many years to grow again. Unless the trail has been recently maintained, you are likely to encounter buckthorn and other shrubs encroaching on the trail in places. As you climb, views of Antelope Valley and Tehachapi Mountains open up to the north.

After 1.9 miles and 800 feet of climbing, reach a small knob marking the southern boundary of the burn area. The trail enters a pleasant forest of black oaks and Coulter pines. Drop down to a small saddle, and then climb steeply as the pines give way to bigcone Douglas fir. The trail soon joins the route of old jeep tracks. In another 1.5 miles, gain the summit ridge and reach a signed junction with the Pacific Crest Trail. The PCT turns left and heads east along the ridge, but your trip continues south on the dirt road past a fence.

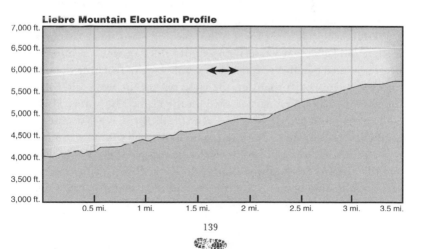

Liebre Mountain Elevation Profile

Note but do *not* follow an unmarked trail on the right immediately beyond the fence.

Continue about 100 yards. The 5,760-foot high point of Liebre Mountain is hidden in a grove of trees on the right, marked by a cairn. There is no view from the summit, and it is covered in foxtail barley, which has unpleasant barbs that catch in your socks; you may wish to skip it unless you are a dedicated peak bagger. (Dog owners should be especially wary because the barbs can get into animals' eyes and cause blindness.) Instead, continue 0.1 mile south to a T-junction with the well-graded Liebre Mountain fire road (Forest Road 7N23). From here, you can enjoy fantastic views over black oaks to the San Gabriel Mountains and Los Padres National Forest.

If you are making an out-and-back trip, this is your turnaround point. If you are making a one-way excursion, begin a scenic walk westward along the ridge. An abandoned segment of the rerouted PCT, now locally known as Golden Eagle Trail, parallels the fire road along the crest of the ridge. You may have seen part of this trail near the fence. Your trip follows the fire road because, at times, the Golden Eagle Trail has been overgrown. However, regular mountain bike traffic may keep the Golden Eagle Trail passable, and adventurous hikers might wish to try exploring it.

Follow the ridge west for 3 miles, passing many dirt roads forking left and right. The western end of the ridge rises to a minor peaklet named Sandberg. A third of a mile before reaching the peak, look for a pair of dirt roads on the right side of the fire road, followed immediately by a narrow trail on the right. This unmarked, easily overlooked path is Golden Eagle Trail. If you reach a spur road on the left leading up to Sandberg, you have gone 0.2 mile too far.

Follow Golden Eagle Trail northwest as it parallels the fire road and then begins descending toward Old Ridge Route. This trail is very popular among mountain bikers, and regular traffic keeps the chaparral at bay. In 2.4 miles, it joins another fire road near Old Ridge Route. Stay left. Pass a short spur on the left leading down to Old Ridge Route, then two more spurs on the right, and emerge at the Sandberg plaque.

DIRECTIONS From Interstate 5 south of the Tejon Pass, exit east on Highway 138. Proceed 4.3 miles to the signed Old Ridge Route at mile marker 138 LA 4.30. Turn right and follow Old Ridge Route south 2.2 miles to a junction with Pine Canyon Rd. If you are planning on a one-way hike, proceed straight up Old Ridge Route for another 0.5 mile to a turnout on the right with a plaque marking the site of the historic Sandberg Inn. Leave a vehicle here and return to Pine Canyon Rd. Turn east onto Pine Canyon and proceed 4.3 miles. At the crest of a hill just beyond mile marker 13.60, turn right (south) onto a rutted dirt road. Follow the road 0.1 mile to its end at the Pacific Crest Trail. If the road is washed out and your vehicle has low clearance, consider parking on the shoulder of Pine Canyon instead.

PERMIT Forest Adventure Pass required.

OTHER POINTS OF INTEREST Antelope Valley California Poppy Reserve located off Highway 138 northeast of Liebre Mountain draws thousands of photographers and sightseers each spring. Wildflower season lasts from mid-February through mid-May and tends to peak in late April. After a rainy winter, the entire landscape lights up with orange poppies, purple lupine, and many other flowers.

The Old Ridge Route, listed on the National Register of Historic Places, opened in 1915 to link the Central Valley to Los Angeles. Considered a miracle of engineering, the twisty road allowed travel as fast as 15 miles per hour. It was superseded by the three-lane US 99 in 1933, then again by the eight-lane Interstate 5 in 1970. In 2005, portions were washed out by a storm and the road is still closed to general use. However, the northern end between Highway 138 and the historic Tumble Inn site is still open to passenger vehicles.

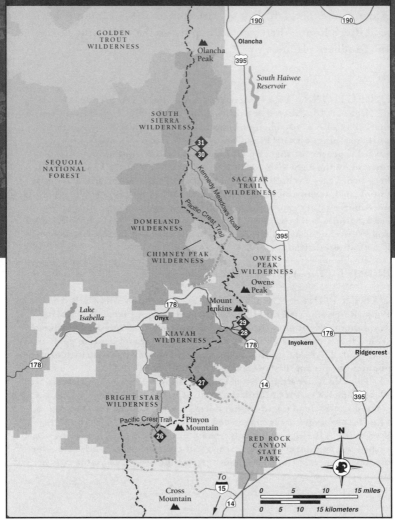

Southern Sierra

GOLDEN TROUT WILDERNESS

Olancha Peak

Olancha

190

190

395

South Haiwee Reservoir

SOUTH SIERRA WILDERNESS

31

30

Kennedy Meadows Road

SEQUOIA NATIONAL FOREST

SACATAR TRAIL WILDERNESS

395

Pacific Crest Trail

DOMELAND WILDERNESS

CHIMNEY PEAK WILDERNESS

OWENS PEAK WILDERNESS

Owens Peak

Lake Isabella

178

Mount Jenkins

Onyx

29

28

178

KIAVAH WILDERNESS

178

Inyokern

178

Ridgecrest

178

27

395

14

BRIGHT STAR WILDERNESS

Pacific Crest Trail

Pinyon Mountain

26

RED ROCK CANYON STATE PARK

N

To

15

14

Cross Mountain

0   5   10   15 miles

0   5   10   15 kilometers

5

SOUTHERN SIERRA

26 Kelso Valley Road to Bird Spring Pass

SCENERY: ✿ ✿ ✿	ELEVATION GAIN: *3,100'*
CHILDREN: ✿	HIKING TIME: *8 hours*
DIFFICULTY: ✿ ✿ ✿ ✿	BEST TIMES: *October–November, March–April*
SOLITUDE: ✿ ✿ ✿ ✿	USFS PCT MAP: *Volume 3*
DISTANCE: *15 miles (one-way)*	OUTSTANDING FEATURES: *Remote desert*

The Southern Sierra is remote, lonesome country spanning high desert and low mountains, with valleys covered in Joshua trees and peaks clad in pinyon pines. You are likely to have the trail to yourself, save for the occasional cow. Although the region is notorious for thoughtless motorcyclists who illegally ride sections of the PCT, this stretch of trail stays off the dirt roads and is less affected by bikers than some nearby sections. Remnants of several abandoned mines can be seen from the trail. In the springtime after a wet winter, you'll enjoy plentiful wildflowers and lively birds. Although the hike lacks the drama of other sections of the PCT, it possesses a certain appeal that will charm the heart of desert lovers.

This trip can be done in either direction but is described from south to north so that the sun is at your back. The trail crosses many dirt roads and motorcycle paths, but is well-marked and the crossings are fortified to discourage motorized vehicles from driving on the PCT. This area is part of the Bureau of Land Management's Jawbone–Butterbredt Area of Critical Environmental Concern. Motorized vehicles are prohibited off of the designated route network, but the still-fresh scars across the desert indicate continued abuse. Bring plenty of water; none is available along the route.

🚶🚶 Mayan Peak is the prominent landmark for the first segment of the hike. From Kelso Valley Rd., hike east through the desert. In 0.3 mile, cross a dirt road. After a sharp turn, you'll see the tailings of St. John Mine on your left. In another 1.6 miles, cross Butterbredt Canyon Rd. (SC 123). The trail follows the southern boulder-studded flank of Mayan Peak and gently climbs into a broad valley dotted with Joshua trees. Peak baggers may select any likely looking route to

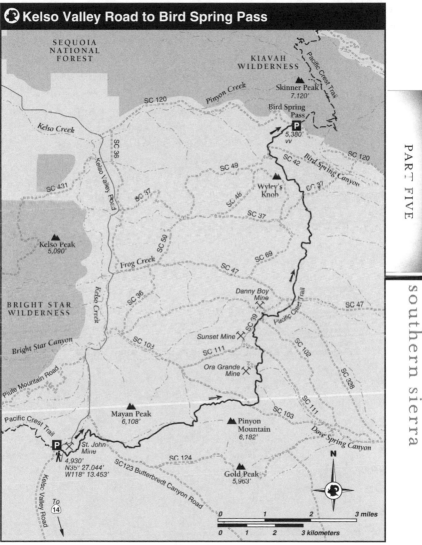

Kelso Valley Road to Bird Spring Pass

SEQUOIA
NATIONAL
FOREST

KIAVAH
WILDERNESS

Pacific Crest Trail

Pinyon Creek

SC 120

Skinner Peak
7,120'

Kelso Creek

Bird Spring
Pass

5,380'
vv

SC 36

Kelso Valley Road

SC 431

SC 37

SC 49

SC 42

Bird Spring Canyon

SC 120

SC 46

Wyley's
Knob

SC 37

SC 37

Kelso Peak
5,090'

SC 50

Frog Creek

SC 47

SC 69

Kelso Creek

BRIGHT STAR
WILDERNESS

SC 36

Danny Boy
Mine

SC 47

SC 103

SC 99

Pacific Crest Trail

SC 102

Bright Star Canyon

Sunset Mine

SC 111

Ora Grande
Mine

SC 328

Piute Mountain Road

Pacific Crest Trail

Mayan Peak
6,108'

St. John
Mine

4,930'
N35° 27.044'
W118° 13.453'

Pinyon
Mountain
6,182'

SC 103

SC 111

Dove Spring Canyon

Kelso Valley Road

To
14

SC123 Butterbredt Canyon Road

SC 124

Gold Peak
5,963'

N

0   1   2   3 miles

0   1   2   3 kilometers

PART FIVE

southern sierra

slog up to the 6,108-foot summit of Mayan Peak; this round-trip adds two miles and 1,500 feet of elevation gain.

In 2.0 more miles, cross a gentle saddle. The vegetation abruptly changes and you will enjoy fine vistas of Pinyon Mountain to the east. The PCT skirts the head of a canyon, curves around the west slope of the mountain, and then leads east across the northern slope. This side earns the mountain its name; the cool, moister slopes support a fine forest of pinyon pines. In 2.1 miles, reach a saddle on the northeast side of the peak where you meet Willow Spring Rd. (SC 103) and a tangle of motorcycle tracks. Water can be found to the west at Willow Spring but is heavily used by cattle and not recommended for humans except in an emergency. (Note that the Forest Service *Pacific Crest National Scenic Trail* map incorrectly shows the PCT on the east side of Pinyon Mountain.)

The next segment parallels SC 39 and crosses a number of dirt roads as it passes a series of mines. As you curve above a drainage stacked with oddly-shaped granite boulders, look back; if the day is clear, you may see the massive form of Mt. Baldy in the distance, draped in snow in the springtime. In 1.7 miles, reach a saddle where

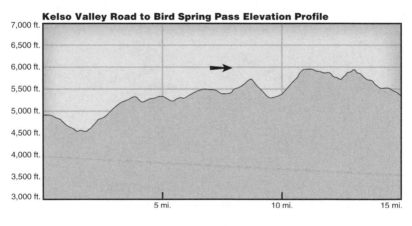

Joshua trees in the southern Sierra

SC 111 crosses the ridge. Off-road vehicles have left many gashes across the desert, areas that are now closed for a lengthy process of regeneration. The trail crosses to the west side of the crest and passes above the ruins of the Ora Grande and Sunset Mines. In 0.8 mile, cross SC 39, and in another 0.2 mile, reach another saddle where SC 102 crosses the ridge. Here you'll see a well-preserved ore chute at Danny Boy gold mine.

Wyley's Knob, crowned by a cluster of radio antennas, comes into view to the north, with Skinner Peak looming over its shoulder. The PCT abruptly descends into a valley and crosses SC 328 in 0.9 mile and then Frog Creek Rd. (SC 47) in another 0.2 mile. It begins a sustained climb up and around the ridge to the north and then follows the ridge to yet another saddle in 3 miles. Here, you'll cross SC 37 and see SC 34 headed northwest to Wyley's Knob.

Curve around the east and north slopes of the knob, passing granite pinnacles and pinyon pines. In 1.7 miles, cross SC 42 just below a service road leading to the knob. Parallel the service road (SC 228) to reach windswept Bird Spring Pass (SC 120) in 0.8 mile. In the event of emergency, you may find a large water cache where the PCT resumes on the north side of the pass. Of historical interest, Bird Spring Pass was first visited by European explorers in 1854, when John Charles Frémont diverted his fifth expedition south because of snow blocking Walker Pass.

DIRECTIONS   Half the fun of this trip is getting to the trailheads. The dirt roads are usually passable by low-clearance vehicles unless they have washed out.

From Highway 14, 0.4 mile north of mile marker 14 KER R35.00 (19.5 miles north of Mojave), turn west onto Jawbone Canyon Rd. Pass the BLM Jawbone Station, and proceed 6.2 miles to the end of the pavement, then another 12.3 miles up the good dirt road to meet Kelso Valley Rd. Turn right (north) on Kelso Valley Rd., and go 5.2 miles to the crest of a ridge where the road becomes paved and you meet the PCT.

Before starting your trip, position a getaway vehicle by continuing north 8.3 miles on Kelso Valley Rd. to a well-marked turnoff on the right for dirt Bird Spring Pass Rd. (SC120), which leads 5.4 miles to a PCT trailhead atop the pass. Then take your other vehicle back to the PCT trailhead on Kelso Valley Rd.

If you would rather bypass the dirt road in Jawbone Canyon, Kelso Valley Rd. can be reached from the north by way of Highway 178 over Walker Pass.

PERMIT   None

OTHER POINTS OF INTEREST   The best option for roadside camping near the trailhead is at the junction of Kelso Valley and Piute Mountain Roads, 2.5 miles north of the southern trailhead.

27 Skinner Peak

SCENERY: ✿ ✿ ✿	ELEVATION GAIN: 1,900'
CHILDREN: ✿ ✿	HIKING TIME: 5 hours
DIFFICULTY: ✿ ✿ ✿	BEST TIMES: October–November, March–April
SOLITUDE: ✿ ✿ ✿ ✿ ✿	USFS PCT MAP: Volume 3
DISTANCE: 8 miles (out–and–back)	OUTSTANDING FEATURES: Remoteness

Skinner Peak (7,120 feet) is the most interesting summit in Kiavah Wilderness, an 88,000-acre wilderness in the Scodie Mountains between Bird Spring Pass and Walker Pass. Climbing Skinner Peak involves a beautiful desert drive to Bird Spring Pass followed by 4 well-graded miles on the PCT and a short cross-country jaunt to the summit. The pinyon-juniper woodlands and desert scrub are appealing to desert lovers, especially during the fall and spring. The peak was named for William Skinner of Wisconsin, who came prospecting for gold and settled in the Kelso Valley. The Scodie Mountains are named for William Scodie, a pioneering merchant who set up shop in nearby Onyx in 1861; his store is believed to be the oldest continuously operating store in California.

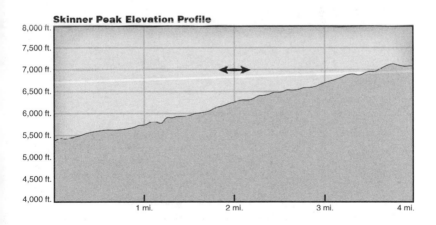

149

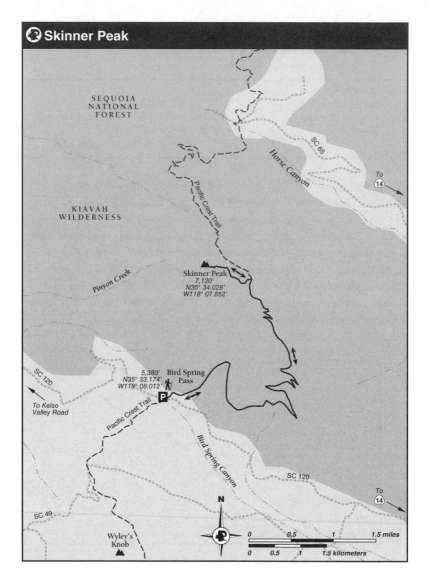

SEQUOIA
NATIONAL
FOREST

Pacific Crest Trail

SC 65

Horse Canyon

To
14

KIAVAH
WILDERNESS

Pinyon Creek

Skinner Peak
7,120'
N35° 34.028'
W118° 07.652'

SC 120

5,380'
N35° 33.174'
W118° 08.012'

Bird Spring
Pass

To Kelso
Valley Road

Pacific Crest Trail

Bird Spring Canyon

SC 120

To
14

SC 49

Wyley's
Knob

N

0   0.5   1   1.5 miles

0   0.5   1   1.5 kilometers

Water cache at Bird Spring Pass

Skinner Peak is one of the rare sections of the PCT between Liebre Mountain and Walker Pass to offer fine hiking. From Liebre Mountain, the trail follows a dusty track along the aqueduct, passes beneath the huge wind farm near Tehachapi, and follows a course overrun by off-road vehicles. Hikers might be tempted to make the 21-mile trek through the Kiavah Wilderness from Bird Spring Pass to Walker Pass, but the middle section has been devastated by fire and follows a road frequented by motorbikes.

The Pacific Crest Trail leads north from Bird Spring Pass toward McIver's Spring and Walker Pass. Near the start of the trail, you will find a cache of emergency water for thru-hikers maintained by a "trail angel" from Weldon. The trail crosses a canyon and then makes broad well-graded switchbacks up the southeast flank of Skinner Peak to reach a ridge in 2.4 miles. It then leads northwest along the ridge.

Pinyon pine

In 0.8 mile, climb some short switchbacks to reach a minor bump overlooking Horse Canyon. On a clear day, you can enjoy panoramic views of Mt. Whitney to the north, Telescope Peak to the northeast, and the San Gabriel Mountains to the south. Backpackers can find sheltered options for dry camping at a flat spot here on the ridge.

In another 0.2 mile, look for a cairn on the left side indicating a convenient departure point for Skinner Peak. Pick a cross-country path through pinyon pines and scrub up to the ridge and westward for 0.4 mile, passing some flat areas and minor rock piles until you reach the distinct summit boulders at the west end of the ridge. Pay close attention on your return so that you don't accidentally drop off the south side of the ridge in the confusing terrain.

DIRECTIONS   This trip requires a long drive on dirt roads. The road is normally graded and passable by low-clearance vehicles unless it has recently washed out. From Highway 14 at call box 14-493 (just north of mile marker 14 KER 49.00 and 33 miles north of Mojave), turn west onto a dirt road signed SC 65. In 4.9 miles, turn left at the covered Los Angeles Aqueduct.

In 0.9 mile, turn right (west) at a junction onto SC 106. Cross another aqueduct. In 2.0 miles, pass a fork on the left for SC 47. In 2.1 miles, turn right (northwest) at a fork onto SC 120. Proceed 4.0 miles to Bird Spring Pass and park.

PERMIT   None

OTHER POINTS OF INTEREST   Bird Spring Pass has adequate space for camping, but the pass forms a funnel for gale-force desert winds.

28 Mount Jenkins

SCENERY: ✿ ✿ ✿ ✿	ELEVATION GAIN: *2,700'*
CHILDREN: ✿	HIKING TIME: *8 hours*
DIFFICULTY: ✿ ✿ ✿	BEST TIMES: *October–May*
SOLITUDE: ✿ ✿ ✿ ✿ ✿	USFS PCT MAP: Volume 3
DISTANCE: *14 miles (out-and-back)*	OUTSTANDING FEATURES: *Views*

Mt. Jenkins (7,921 feet) is one of the most accessible and enjoyable peaks along the Pacific Crest Trail in the southern Sierra Nevada. It was named for James Jenkins, a prolific young naturalist who wrote the authoritative guidebooks to the southern Sierra before being killed on his way to the mountains by an erratic driver. This trip involves a 6.3-mile hike on the PCT from Walker Pass, followed by a 0.6-mile walk up a good climber's trail.

🚶🚶 From Walker Pass, begin hiking north on the PCT. You will immediately see a trail register and cross the Owens Peak Wilderness boundary. The PCT follows the desert slopes above a magnificent forest of Joshua trees. In 1.2 miles, the trail begins switchbacking, climbing up to the Sierra Crest where you enter a forest of pinyon pines.

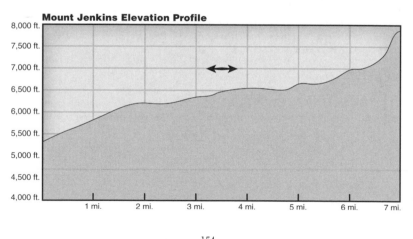

Mount Jenkins Elevation Profile

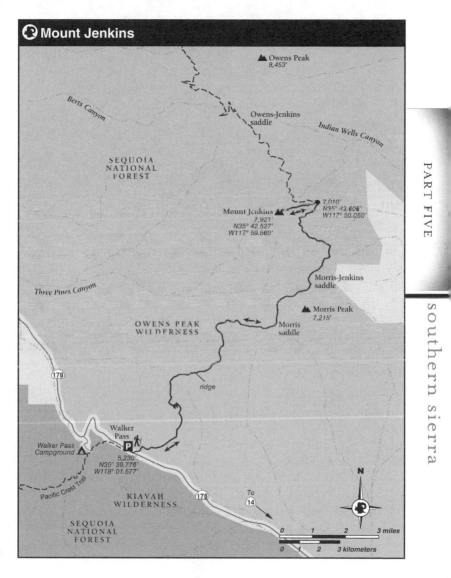

Owens Peak
8,453'

Berts Canyon

Owens-Jenkins
saddle

Indian Wells Canyon

SEQUOIA
NATIONAL
FOREST

7,010'
N35° 42.606'
W117° 59.059'

Mount Jenkins
7,921'
N35° 42.527'
W117° 59.569'

Three Pines Canyon

Morris-Jenkins
saddle

Morris Peak
7,215'

OWENS PEAK
WILDERNESS

Morris
saddle

178

ridge

Walker
Pass
P

Walker Pass
Campground

5,230'
N35° 39.776'
W118° 01.577'

Pacific Crest Trail

KIAVAH
WILDERNESS

178

To
14

SEQUOIA
NATIONAL
FOREST

N

0   1   2   3 miles

0   1   2   3 kilometers

PART FIVE

southern sierra

Approaching the summit of Mt. Jenkins

Reach the crest in 0.7 mile and cross to the west side, where you get your first view of Domeland Wilderness to the northwest. Follow the crest for 2.0 miles to a saddle south of Morris Peak. The origin of the peak's name is unknown; some speculate that Mr. Morris might have been a member of the team that first surveyed the area. Hikers looking for a longer trip can follow a use trail up the south ridge to the summit; this excursion adds 0.5 mile each way and 630 feet of climbing.

The trail winds around the west side of Morris for 0.8 mile to the Morris–Jenkins saddle and then crosses to the east side of Jenkins.

In another 0.2 mile, look for a plaque commemorating Jim Jenkins, who died in 1979 at age 27. The mountain was named in his memory in 1984.

The trail gradually climbs, curving around the southeast ridge of Mt. Jenkins to reach views of the granite battlements of Owens Ridge. In July 2010 1,800 acres of the area burned in the Owens Peak Complex Fire. Watch for large nolinas, whose sharp blades are easily mistaken for yuccas. This is the only place in the Sierra Nevada where the remarkable plants can be found.

In 1.4 miles, reach the east ridge of Mt. Jenkins. A cairn marks the start of a good 0.6-mile climber's trail to the summit. The first part of the climber's trail passes through a ghostly forest of charred pinyon pines but soon escapes the burn area. The trail follows the ridge to a point just below the intimidating blocks forming the jagged peak. Watch for cairns marking the path; staying on the trail is definitely worth the effort. The path traverses left onto the face and follows a clever path between the rocks to the crest. Turn left and scramble up the rocks to the summit.

southern sierra

DIRECTIONS From Highway 14, turn west onto Highway 178 and drive 8.5 miles to Walker Pass. Park on a dirt frontage road on the north side of the pass.

PERMIT None

OTHER POINTS OF INTEREST The Walker Pass Campground 1 mile west of the pass provides free camping on a first-come, first-served basis. Water is not available.

29 Owens Peak Wilderness

SCENERY: ⛰ ⛰ ⛰ ⛰ ⛰
CHILDREN: ⛰
DIFFICULTY: ⛰ ⛰ ⛰ ⛰ ⛰
SOLITUDE: ⛰ ⛰ ⛰ ⛰ ⛰
DISTANCE: *28 miles (one-way)*
ELEVATION GAIN: *4,800'*

HIKING TIME: *2–3 days*
BEST TIMES: *April–May, October–November*
USFS PCT MAP: Volume 3
OUTSTANDING FEATURES: *Granite peaks and seclusion*

The Sierra Nevada give their southernmost hint of their full granitic glory near Owens Peak. This trip from Walker Pass to Chimney Creek Campground follows the crest past awe-inspiring buttresses and spires, dipping down to seek water and then regaining the ridge. The 74,000-acre Owens Peak Wilderness was established in 1994 as part of the Desert Protection Act. Owens Peak (and the nearby Owens Valley and Owens Lake) was named by explorer John Charles Frémont for Richard Owens, a member of his third expedition. However, Owens probably never saw his namesake peak.

This area is covered with snow and ice in the winter and bakes under the desert sun during the summer, so it is best visited in spring and fall. Few people other than PCT thru-hikers discover this beautiful backpacking trip; you may have the trail entirely to yourself. The fall is deer season, and while most hunters stay in the valleys below, it is prudent to wear bright clothing.

Backpackers will find pleasant camping opportunities every hour or two, including at all water sources and at each saddle along the ridge. However, water is only available at Joshua Tree Spring and possibly at Spanish Needle Creek. *Plan to carry at least four quarts of water, or more in the warmer months. In the fall, when Spanish Needle Creek is unreliable, the best option is a two-day trip camping near Joshua Tree Spring, with a long second day. In the spring, it is possible to make a three-day trip. Stay at Joshua Tree Spring on the first night. On the second day, fill your water at Spanish Needle Creek and climb to the Lamont-Spanish Needle saddle for a spectacular dry camp.*

Dedicated peak baggers may wish to test their mettle on some of the summits along the way, including Morris Peak, Mt. Jenkins, Owens Peak, Lamont Peak, Spanish Needle,

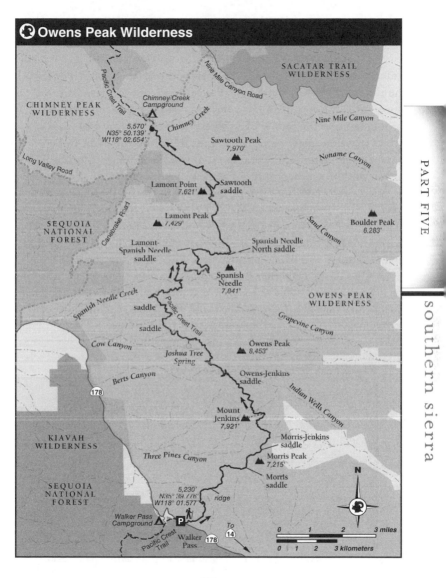

Owens Peak Wilderness

SACATAR TRAIL WILDERNESS

Nine Mile Canyon Road

CHIMNEY PEAK WILDERNESS

Pacific Crest Trail

Chimney Creek Campground

5,570'
N35° 50.139'
W118° 02.654'

Chimney Creek

Nine Mile Canyon

Sawtooth Peak
7,970'

Noname Canyon

Long Valley Road

Lamont Point
7,021'

Sawtooth saddle

SEQUOIA NATIONAL FOREST

Canebrake Road

Lamont Peak
7,429'

Spanish Needle North saddle

Sand Canyon

Boulder Peak
6,283'

Lamont-Spanish Needle saddle

Spanish Needle
7,841'

Spanish Needle Creek

saddle

Pacific Crest Trail

OWENS PEAK WILDERNESS

Grapevine Canyon

saddle

Cow Canyon

Joshua Tree Spring

Owens Peak
8,453'

Berts Canyon

Owens-Jenkins saddle

Indian Wells Canyon

178

Mount Jenkins
7,921'

KIAVAH WILDERNESS

Three Pines Canyon

Morris-Jenkins saddle

Morris Peak
7,215'

Morris saddle

SEQUOIA NATIONAL FOREST

5,230'
N35° 39.778'
W118° 01.577'

ridge

N

Walker Pass Campground

P

To
14

Pacific Crest Trail

Walker Pass

178

0   1   2   3 miles

0   1   2   3 kilometers

Lamont Point, or Sawtooth Peak. Consult Exploring the Southern Sierra: East *by Jim and Ruby Jenkins for details.*

From Walker Pass, begin hiking north on the PCT. You will immediately see a trail register and cross the Owens Peak Wilderness boundary. The PCT follows the desert slopes above a magnificent forest of Joshua trees. In 1.2 miles, the trail begins switchbacking, climbing up to the Sierra Crest where you enter a forest of pinyon pines that dominate the vegetation for the rest of the trip. In September and October, the ripe pine nuts make a delicious trail snack if you can extract them without getting coated in sap.

Reach the crest in 0.7 mile and cross to the west side, where you get your first view of Domeland Wilderness to the northwest. The bulk of your first day's climb is now done. Follow the crest for 2.0 miles to a saddle south of Morris Peak. The origin of the peak's name is unknown; some speculate that Mr. Morris might have been a member of the team that first surveyed the area. The trail winds around the west side of Morris for 0.8 mile to the Morris-Jenkins saddle and then crosses to the east side of Jenkins. In another 0.2 mile, look for a plaque commemorating Jim Jenkins.

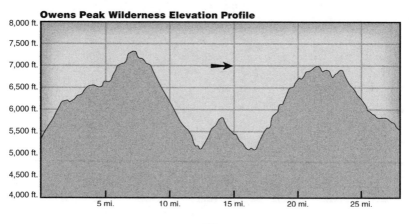

Owens Peak Wilderness Elevation Profile

The trail gradually climbs, curving around the southeast ridge of Mt. Jenkins to give the first views of the impressive Owens Ridge. The pinnacles at the far eastern end of the Owens Ridge are called the Five Fingers. Watch for large nolinas, whose sharp blades are easily mistaken for yuccas. This is the only place in the Sierra Nevada where the remarkable plants can be found. In July 2010 1,800 acres of this area burned in the Owens Peak Complex Fire. In 1.4 miles, reach the east ridge of Mt. Jenkins. A cairn marks the start of a good climber's trail to the summit (see Hike 28, page 154). The PCT continues northwest across the steep mountainside above Indian Wells Canyon. In 0.8 mile, reach a corner with a dramatic view of Owens Peak. In another 1.4 miles, come to the Owens-Jenkins saddle.

Nolinas

At this point, the PCT departs the Sierra Crest in search of water. Make a long switchback down from the saddle. Watch for glimpses of Lake Isabella to the west. In 1.4 miles, cross another minor saddle, and take a well-graded descent into Cow Canyon. Cross two minor dry creek beds on the canyon floor. The pinyon pines give way to Joshua trees. You may spot traces of an old jeep road that work crews once used for trail access while building the PCT. It has been closed and is now returning to its natural state.

In 1.8 miles, reach a sign indicating Joshua Tree Spring to the left. Most parties will want to refill their water bottles here. Follow the quarter-mile trail steeply down past a pair of campsites into a ravine. The spring is just below two more campsites in the bottom of the ravine beneath canyon live oaks. By the end of the season, the unmaintained spring may have diminished to a trickle. Be sure to treat the water before drinking it. According to the Bureau of Land Management, the water exceeds federal standards for uranium, though hikers use the spring regularly. Since the spring attracts much insect life, the higher campsites may be more pleasant. Take care storing your food; backpackers have encountered bears here.

The PCT continues northwest across more dry creek beds to cross a minor saddle in 1.2 miles. It then climbs northward to a larger saddle in another 1.4 miles. At this point, you depart the Cow Canyon drainage and enter the watershed of Spanish Needle Creek. Look for the granite battlements of Lamont Peak directly to the north. Far to the west is the slash of Canebrake Rd. The trail switchbacks down and then leads east. Look for the jagged towers of Spanish Needle at the head of the canyon to the east. Although it is not named on topographic maps, Spanish Needle is one of the most noteworthy summits in the southern Sierra, and its rocky summit is coveted by mountaineers.

In 1.8 miles, cross the southernmost fork of Spanish Needle Creek beneath the live oaks where you might find water in the spring. In 0.4 mile, reach the main fork of the creek. This source is considered reliable, but may still dry up by late fall. A fine campsite is hidden on a bench just before reaching the creek crossing. You are now at the lowest elevation along the entire hike. The trail begins climbing to cross a third fork of Spanish Needle Creek in 0.7 mile. This spring-fed stream often contains water even when the others are

Boundless enthusiasm at Spanish Needle saddle

dry. If you don't find water and lack an adequate supply to complete the remaining 12 miles of the PCT, your only option for escape is to hike west down Spanish Needle Canyon to Canebrake Rd. The bottom of the canyon is private property signed NO TRESPASSING; use this exit only for emergencies.

The PCT now makes a long, well-graded 1,500-foot ascent to the Lamont–Spanish Needle saddle. In 0.8 mile, recross the creek drainage, where you may find wild roses and columbine. Watch for the numerous beavertail cactus along the route. In 2.6 miles, reach the saddle. You'll find many fine campsites under the pinyon pines on both sides of the trail; these sites were originally used by the PCT trail crew building the trail.

The trail turns east along the north slopes of Spanish Needle. These cooler slopes hold moisture longer and support a different

Lamont Peak and Meadow

variety of trees, including sugar and Jeffrey pines, white firs, and black oaks. In 1.1 miles, reach another saddle with views of Spanish Needle's massive spires. Bold mountaineers have been known to climb the peak from here, but the ascent involves intricate route-finding and third-class climbing on the summit rocks. Turn north again and follow the west side of the crest for 2.1 miles toward the next granite-topped mountain, locally known as Lamont Point. The various Lamont names were given by the MacFadden family, nineteenth-century landholders in the valley, to remember their former home in Scotland. Look back for splendid views of the Lamont Pinnacles above Lamont Meadow. After passing the head of Sand Canyon, reach a saddle southeast of Lamont Point. The trail now descends northward, making a short switchback and a much longer switchback before reaching the saddle south of Sawtooth Peak in 1.3 miles. Watch for magnificent western junipers on these shaded slopes.

Turn northwest for the final gradual descent. Graceful gray pines become plentiful in this canyon. They are most common in the foothills ringing the Central Valley; this grove near Sawtooth Peak represents the extreme upper elevation range of the species. Their huge, ferocious cones are easily confused for Coulter pinecones. Native Americans opened the cones with fire to harvest the large nuts, which were prized for their high protein and fat content. In 0.8 mile, cross a seasonal creek. In another 2.4 miles, cross a jeep road and Chimney Creek near the edge of Lamont Meadow, and then hike through a field of rabbit bush to reach the end of your hike at Canebrake Rd. If your ride waits at Chimney Creek Campground, turn north on the road and walk 0.3 mile to the campground entrance.

DIRECTIONS   This trip requires a 20-mile car shuttle.

From Highway 14, 2.8 miles south of the junction with Highway 395, turn west onto Highway 178 and drive 8.5 miles to Walker Pass, where your trip begins. However, you may first need to position a getaway vehicle at the northern trailhead.

To do so, continue west 9 miles. Pass mile marker 178 KER 71.00, then in 0.4 mile turn right (north) on graded dirt Canebrake Rd. at a sign for Chimney Peak Special Recreation Management Area. Proceed 10.8 miles to the intersection of the PCT with Canebrake Rd, where you may park the second vehicle in a small turnout. Return to Walker Pass to begin your trip.

If you are concerned about the safety of your vehicle, you may prefer to start at Walker Pass Campground and end at Chimney Creek Campground. Walker Pass Campground is 1 mile west of the pass on Highway 178 near mile marker 178 KER 79.00. The PCT passes the campground and adds 0.6 mile to your trip. Chimney Creek Campground is 0.3 mile north of the PCT on Canebrake Rd. Both of these campgrounds are free and do not take reservations. *Bring your own water.*

PERMIT   None

30 Kennedy Meadows to Kern River Bridge

SCENERY: ✿ ✿ ✿
CHILDREN: ✿ ✿ ✿ ✿
DIFFICULTY: ✿
SOLITUDE: ✿ ✿
DISTANCE: *4 miles (out–and–back)*
ELEVATION GAIN: *150'*
HIKING TIME: *2 hours*

BEST TIMES: *May–October*
TOM HARRISON MAP: South Sierra
Wilderness
USFS PCT MAP: Volume 3
OUTSTANDING FEATURES: *Kern River and picnicking*

This family–friendly hike follows the Kern River from Kennedy Meadows Campground to the bridge across the river. Kids will enjoy the opportunities to picnic, play near the river, or collect pine nuts along the trail. This destination makes for an easy introductory backpacking trip. Parents should teach their children a healthy respect for the power of the river, especially during spring runoff.

🚶🚶 The signed Pacific Crest Trail starts at the north end of the Kennedy Meadows Campground loop. Follow the trail north along

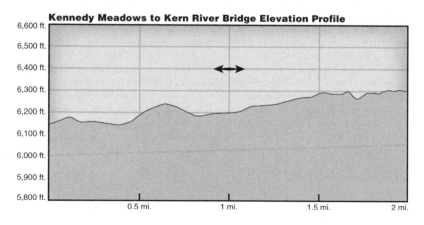

Kennedy Meadows to Kern River Bridge Elevation Profile

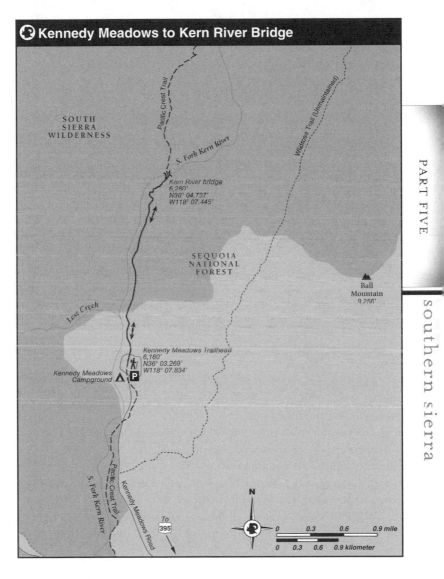

Kennedy Meadows to Kern River Bridge

SOUTH
SIERRA
WILDERNESS

Pacific Crest Trail

S. Fork Kern River

Wildrose Trail (Unmaintained)

Kern River bridge
6,280'
N36° 04.737'
W118° 07.445'

SEQUOIA
NATIONAL
FOREST

Ball
Mountain
9,256'

Lost Creek

Kennedy Meadows Trailhead
6,160'
N36° 03.269'
W118° 07.834'

Kennedy Meadows
Campground

Pacific Crest Trail

S. Fork Kern River

Kennedy Meadows Road

To
395

N

| 0 | 0.3 | 0.6 | 0.9 mile |
| 0 | 0.3 | 0.6 | 0.9 kilometer |

PCT bridge over the Kern River

the east bank of the Kern River. There are many opportunities to
veer off the trail and visit the river.

Pinyon pines dominate the forest at this elevation. In September
and October, the cones are heavily laden with large nuts. It is legal
to gather reasonable quantities for personal use in the national forest without a permit. Once you have removed the nut from the sappy
cones, crack the shell and extract the tiny nut. The raw nuts are tasty to
eat on the trail, though some people prefer them lightly roasted. These
pine nuts were a seasonally important component of Native American diets and a cause for great celebration. Given that a thousand nuts

weigh about one pound, the gatherers were incredibly skilled to be able to collect a nutritionally significant quantity of nuts.

In 0.4 mile, another sign marks the entrance to the South Sierra Wilderness. Look for Lost Creek coming out of a canyon to the west. Pass a number of shady spots attractive for picnics or camping. In another 1.5 miles, reach the sturdy bridge over the Kern River. This bridge is essential for PCT hikers to safely cross the river when snowmelt turns the river into a raging torrent.

The PCT continues north to Clover Meadow and Monache Meadow (see Hike 31, page 170), but you've seen the most attractive portion. This is a fine place to rest and enjoy the scenery before retracing your steps to the campground.

DIRECTIONS   From Highway 395 north of Inyokern at mile marker 395 INY R 3.00, turn west onto Nine Mile Canyon Rd. At the head of the canyon, the road changes name to Kennedy Meadows Rd. (J41). When you reach the Kennedy Meadows General Store, 24.2 miles from the highway, stay right and follow signs 2.6 miles north to Kennedy Meadows Campground. Camping is presently $17 per night, but hikers can park free in a large lot adjacent to the PCT trailhead at the north end of the campground.

PERMIT   None

31 South Sierra Wilderness

SCENERY: ✿ ✿ ✿ ✿	BEST TIMES: *June–October*
CHILDREN: ✿	TOM HARRISON MAP: *South Sierra*
DIFFICULTY: ✿ ✿ ✿	*Wilderness*
SOLITUDE: ✿ ✿ ✿ ✿	USFS PCT MAP: *Volume 3*
DISTANCE: *23 miles (one–way with shuttle)*	OUTSTANDING FEATURES: *River, meadows,*
ELEVATION GAIN: *3,900'*	*and high plateau*
HIKING TIME: *13 hours or 2–3 days*	

The South Sierra Wilderness, established by Congress in 1984, is a 63,000-acre section of the Sierra Nevada on the high plateau of the Kern River sandwiched between Golden Trout Wilderness and Domeland Wilderness. This backpacking trip leads from Kennedy Meadows to Olancha Pass through the heart of the wilderness. It passes the Wild and Scenic South Fork of the Kern River, vast alpine meadows, and rugged peaks. The wilderness is lightly visited, and the Pacific Crest Trail accounts for the great majority of hiker traffic through the region. The area gets hot in the summer and is covered in snow for most of the winter; the ideal time to visit is late spring or early fall. Beware that the fall deer season draws hunters to the Southern Sierra.

This hike is described south-to-north, which involves a long, gradual ascent. If you like to get nearly all of your elevation gain out of the way at the start, you might prefer to start at Olancha Pass and head southward. Backpackers on a two-day trip will likely choose to camp near the Kern River bridge in Monache Meadow. Those on a three-day trip may have a challenge finding campsites near water in the fall. The best options may be to fill up bottles at the headwaters of Crag Creek and camp just south of Beck Meadow, and then camp a second night near a creek at the junction of the PCT and the Olancha Pass Trail.

🏃🏃 From the signed PCT trailhead at the north end of Kennedy Meadows Campground, hike north along the east bank of the Kern River. This is a popular area for families to picnic and play along the river (see Hike 30, page 166). You soon pass a sign marking your entrance into the South Sierra Wilderness. In 1.9 miles, reach the bridge over the South Fork of the Kern River. In the fall, this river

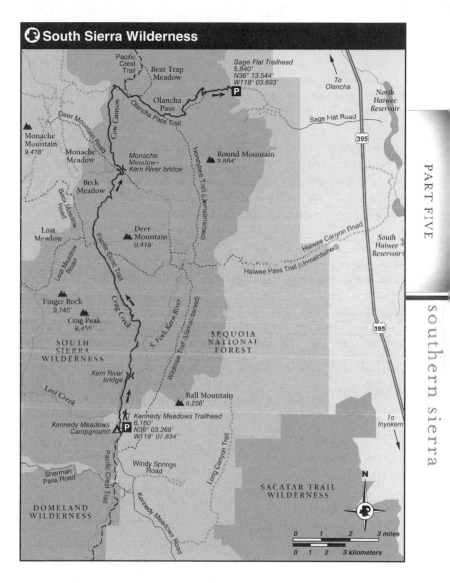

South Sierra Wilderness

Pacific Crest Trail

Bear Trap Meadow

Sage Flat Trailhead
5,840'
N36° 13.544'
W118° 03.693'

To Olancha

North Haiwee Reservoir

Olancha Pass

Olancha Pass Trail

Sage Flat Road

Deer Mountain Road

Cow Canyon

395

Monache Mountain
9,418'

Monache Meadow

Monache Meadow–Kern River bridge

Round Mountain
9,884'

Horrelbee Trail (Unmaintained)

Beck Meadow

Beck Meadow Road

Lost Meadow

Lost Meadow Road

Pacific Crest Trail

Deer Mountain
9,418'

Haiwee Canyon Road

South Haiwee Reservoir

Haiwee Pass Trail (Unmaintained)

Finger Rock
9,145'

Crag Peak
9,455'

Crag Creek

SOUTH SIERRA WILDERNESS

S. Fork Kern River

Wildrose Trail (Unmaintained)

SEQUOIA NATIONAL FOREST

Kern River bridge

Lost Creek

Ball Mountain
9,256'

To Inyokern

Kennedy Meadows Trailhead
6,160'
N36° 03.269'
W118° 07.834'

Kennedy Meadows Campground

395

Long Canyon Trail

Windy Springs Road

Sherman Pass Road

Pacific Crest Trail

DOMELAND WILDERNESS

Kennedy Meadows Road

SACATAR TRAIL WILDERNESS

N

0   1   2   3 miles
0   1   2   3 kilometers

may be your last reliable water source before you reach the Kern again 10 miles up the trail in Monache Meadow.

The river veers east into a canyon, but the PCT continues north around the west side of a minor peak. This area was once heavily used by stock, and you may still find traces of the old stock paths. Reach a saddle at the north side of the peak in 1.2 miles. The trail makes one switchback, and then weaves along the hillside to cross Crag Creek (dry in the fall) in 0.7 mile. The Clover Fire, started by lightning in May 2008, burned for nearly two months and consumed 15,000 acres of forest between Crag Creek and Beck Meadow. The charred Jeffrey pines stand in bleak contrast to the healthy pinyon pine forest along the Kern River.

The trail follows the east edge of Clover Meadow and climbs a long drainage to a saddle in 3.6 miles. You may find water in the creek high up in the drainage even if it is dry near the meadow. The Haiwee Pass Trail (37E01) departs east from the saddle, but this trip continues north on the PCT. You soon exit the burn area and find pleasant dry campsites in the soft duff beneath the lodgepole pines.

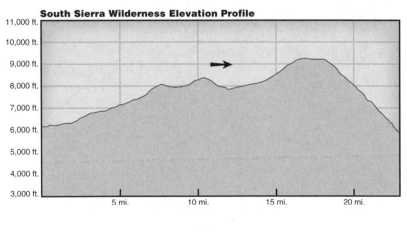

South Sierra Wilderness Elevation Profile

Descend to the edge of Beck Meadow, the southern offshoot of the expansive Monache Meadow. In 0.5 mile, stay right at a trail junction at the edge of the meadow. Enjoy the terrific views of the meadow and the bare peaks of the High Sierra beyond. Since the days of the Old West, ranchers have driven their cattle to forage in Monache Meadow each summer. These historic grazing rights persist despite the wilderness designation and the fragile nature of the alpine meadows. Although you will see a creek and springs along the meadow, the water quality is dubious because of the heavy cattle presence.

In another 0.5 mile, stay right again at a fork. Gradually climb across the northwest flank of Deer Mountain. Look back for great views of Crag Peak and Finger Rock over the meadow. In 1.0 mile, pass a cattle gate. Ahead, look for Olancha Peak, the southernmost of the great Sierra peaks. In 0.7 mile, cross a minor ridge. Dry camping is available here, but most hikers will prefer to continue to the Kern River. The PCT leaves the forest and descends open slopes to cross a defunct jeep trail in 1.1 miles. Before this area was designated wilderness, jeeps and off-road vehicles ran rampant over the high plateau, but this unsustainable use has largely ceased. In another 0.4 mile, reach the Kern River again. During peak spring runoff, the Kern River presents a formidable barrier to hikers. A sturdy bridge was built across the river in 1986 to aid PCT hikers. There is fine camping beneath the trees on the south side and plenty of soft but exposed camping on the sandy field on the north. Camp at least 100 feet from the water; don't disturb the delicate grassy banks of the river.

A maze of trails radiates from this point; you should follow the well-signed PCT north toward the mouth of Cow Canyon. In 2.0 miles, pass an easy-to-miss trail leading south back to the meadow. Continue up the canyon, repeatedly crossing the creek and passing traces of old stock trails. In 1.8 miles, reach a signed junction at the top of the canyon. The left fork goes to Monache Meadow, but

this trip turns right (east) toward Olancha Pass. In 0.4 mile, reach
a second signed junction. Leave the PCT at this point, and take the
southeast-bound Olancha Pass Trail. There are a number of camping options here with a creek nearby, although water may not be reliable in the fall. In another 0.4 mile, pass a connector trail for the
PCT near the edge of Summit Meadow. Hike along the north edge of
the long, narrow meadow, passing a corral and packer's camp. Heavy
use by stock has worn the trail down to a sandy groove in places. In
1.4 miles, reach the lonely, windswept Olancha Pass.

The little-used Honeybee Trail leads south along the Sierra
Crest toward Haiwee Pass, but this trip starts the long descent of the
pass to the east. Enjoy the fantastic views of the desert and the rugged
slopes of Olancha. In 1.0 mile, cross a small saddle. The cow trail

Olancha Pass

goes straight down the canyon, but most people will prefer to stay on the hiker trail, which makes more gradual switchbacks. In 2.5 miles, the trails rejoin near the canyon floor. In 0.7 mile, pass a gate. The trail soon deteriorates into a confusing web of paths. Stay above the fence line to reach a sign marking the edge of the South Sierra Wilderness in 0.1 mile. Then follow the better-defined trail as it switchbacks and reaches the Olancha Pass Trailhead in 0.5 mile.

VARIATION Upon study of the map, adventurous hikers will find multiple options for loop hikes through the South Sierra Wilderness.

DIRECTIONS This trip requires a 59-mile car shuttle. From Highway 395 north of Inyokern, arrange one vehicle at the Sage Flat Trailhead for Olancha Pass, then drive a second to Kennedy Meadows Trailhead.

To reach Sage Flat, drive north on Highway 395 and turn left (west) on paved Sage Flat Rd. just before mile marker 395 INY R 29.5 (5 miles south of the small town of Olancha). Proceed 3.3 miles to the end of the pavement, and then continue 2.2 miles on a graded dirt road, passing several minor side roads. Drive past the corral and equestrian parking to the hiker parking by the trailhead marker at the road's end.

Return to Highway 395 and drive south for 26.4 miles. Then turn right (west) onto Nine Mile Canyon Rd. at mile marker 395 INY R 3.00. At the head of the canyon, the road changes name to Kennedy Meadows Rd. (J41). When you reach the Kennedy Meadows General Store, 24.2 miles from the highway, stay right and follow signs 2.6 miles north to Kennedy Meadows Campground. Camping is presently $17 per night, but hikers can park free in a large lot adjacent to the PCT trailhead at the north end of the campground.

PERMIT This trip does not require a wilderness permit or adventure pass. However, the Forest Service limits groups to 15 people and 25 heads of stock within the South Sierra Wilderness.

Olancha Peak (Hike 31)

Appendix: Managing Agencies

ANGELES NATIONAL FOREST
Los Angeles River Ranger District
12371 N. Little Tujunga Canyon Rd.
San Fernando, CA 91342
(818) 899-1900
Hike 22

Santa Clara and Mojave Rivers Ranger District
33708 Crown Valley Rd.
Acton, CA 93510
(661) 296-9710
Hikes 19–21 and 25

ANZA-BORREGO DESERT STATE PARK
200 Palm Canyon Dr.
Borrego Springs, CA 92004
(760) 767-5311
Hike 7

BUREAU OF LAND MANAGEMENT
Palm Springs: South Coast Field Office
1201 Bird Center Dr.
Palm Springs, CA 92262
(760) 833-7100
Hike 1

Ridgecrest Field Office
300 S. Richmond Rd.
Ridgecrest, CA 93555
(760) 384-5400
Hikes 26–29

(Continued on next page)

Cleveland National Forest

Descanso Ranger District
10845 Ranch Bernardo Rd., Suite 200
San Diego, CA 92127
(858) 673-6180
Hikes 2—4

Palomar Ranger District
10845 Ranch Bernardo Rd., Suite 200
San Diego, CA 92127
(760) 788-0250
Hikes 5—6

San Bernardino National Forest

Arrowhead Ranger Station
28104 Highway 18
P.O. Box 350
Skyforest, CA 92385
(909) 382-2782
Hikes 17—18

Big Bear Discovery Center
40971 North Shore Dr.
Fawnskin, CA 92333
(909) 382-2790
Hikes 14—16

San Jacinto and Santa Rosa Mountains National Monument

Idyllwild Ranger Station
54270 Pine Crest
P.O. Box 518
Idyllwild, CA 92549
(909) 328-2921
Hikes 8—12

SEQUOIA NATIONAL FOREST
Kernville Ranger Station
105 Whitney Rd.
Kernville, CA 93238
(760) 376-3781
Hikes 30–31

VASQUEZ ROCKS COUNTY PARK
10700 West Escondido Canyon Rd.
Agua Dulce, CA 91390
(661) 268-0840
Hike 24

WILDLANDS CONSERVANCY
Whitewater Preserve Ranger Station
(760) 325-7222

Mission Creek Preserve
(760) 369-7105
Hike 13

managing agencies

Bibliography

PCT Guidebooks

Asorson, "Erik the Black." *Pacific Crest Trail Atlas*, 3rd edition, vols. 1–2. Blackwoods Press, 2012. *Just the facts: maps, mileage, water, camping, and resupply points in a compact package.*

Schifrin, Ben, Jeffrey Schaffer, Thomas Winnett, and Ruby Jenkins. *Pacific Crest Trail: Southern California*, 6th edition. Berkeley: Wilderness Press, 2003. *The classic PCT guidebook, with extensive information on the flora, geology, history, and sights along the trail.*

Regional Hiking Guides

For those interested in more hikes in each of the regions of this guide, the following comprehensive books offer the best coverage of each area:

Harris, David, and Jennifer Money Harris. *Afoot and Afield: Inland Empire*. Berkeley: Wilderness Press, 2009. *Parts 2 and 3: San Jacinto and San Bernardino Mountains.*

Jenkins, J. C., and Ruby Jenkins. *Exploring the Southern Sierra: East Side*. Berkeley: Wilderness Press, 1992. *Part 5: Southern Sierra Nevada.*

Schad, Jerry. *Afoot and Afield: Los Angeles County*. 3rd edition. Berkeley: Wilderness Press, 2009. *Part 4: San Gabriel Mountains.*

———. *Afoot and Afield: San Diego County*. 4th edition. Berkeley: Wilderness Press, 2007. *Part 1: San Diego.*

GPS Navigation

Hinch, Stephen. *Outdoor Navigation with GPS*. 3rd edition: Berkeley: Wilderness Press, 2010.

Trail Adventures

Ballard, Angela, and Duffy Ballard. *A Blistered Kind of Love: One Couple's Trial by Trail*. Seattle: Mountaineers Books, 2003. *A young couple tells an entertaining story of their adventures on the PCT.*

Hughes, Rees, and Corey Lee Lewis, eds. *The Pacific Crest Trailside Reader: California*. Seattle: Mountaineers Books, 2011. *An anthology of stories and essays that gives a terrific feel for the famed trail from dozens of points of view.*

Ryback, Eric. *The High Adventures of Eric Ryback: Canada to Mexico on Foot*. San Francisco: Chronicle Books, 1971. *A colorful tale from the PCT's first thru-hiker.*

Strayed, Cheryl. *Wild: From Lost to Found on the Pacific Crest Trail*. NYC: Knopf, 2012. *A young woman impulsively seeks redemption on the trail after her life crumbles.*

Index

About the Author

DAVID MONEY HARRIS has been roaming the California mountains since he was but a wee tot in his father's backpack. Later, he fell in love with the Sierra Nevada on Boy Scout backpacking trips and as a leader in the Sierra Club's Peak Climbing Section. During the past thirteen years, he has explored the amazingly diverse mountains of Southern California. For much of the past seven years, his own three sons have been riding along on these adventures.

David teaches engineering at Harvey Mudd College in Claremont, California. He is also the coauthor of *Afoot & Afield Inland Empire* and *San Bernardino Mountain Trails.* When he is not teaching or on the trail, he can be found in Upland with his wife Jennifer and their sons.

Taking care of the Pacific Crest Trail is a full-time effort.

The Pacific Crest Trail Association's mission is to protect, preserve and promote the trail as a resource for hikers and equestrians and for the value that wild lands provide to all people.

Through a formal partnership with the U.S. Forest Service, our nonprofit membership organization is the primary caretaker of this 2,650-mile National Scenic Trail as it winds through the American West's most beautiful landscapes.

Each year, PCTA volunteers and paid staff members clear downed trees and repair washed out tread. We monitor threats to the trail and speak up on its behalf. We tell the trail's story in print and online. And we advocate for federal support by visiting our elected leaders in Washington, D.C.

All this effort safeguards the experiences and solitude people deserve when they venture into the wild.

Please help preserve this national treasure for future generations by joining the PCTA.

Your $35 annual membership will ensure that this trail will never end.

Photo by Josh Meier

1331 Garden Highway
Sacramento, CA 95833
(916) 285-1846
www.pcta.org • info@pcta.org

PACIFIC CREST TRAIL
ASSOCIATION